Teaching Young Children in Violent Times:

BUILDING A PEACEABLE CLASSROOM

Teaching Young Children in Violent Times: Building a Peaceable Classroom
Second Edition
By Diane E. Levin, Ph.D.

© Copyright 1994 and 2003 Educators for Social Responsibility
All rights reserved. Published 2003.
Printed in the United States of America

Levin, Diane E.
ISBN 0-942349-18-0

Co-published with:
National Association for the Education of Young Children
1509 16th Street NW
Washington, DC 20036
www.naeyc.org

Inquiries regarding permission to reprint all or part of this book
should be addressed to:
Permissions Editor
Educators for Social Responsibility
23 Garden Street
Cambridge, MA 02138
www.esrnational.org

Cover and book design: schwadesign, Boston, MA
Cover background image: Photodisc/Getty Images
Interior product photography: Deirdra Funcheon

This book is printed on recycled paper.

Teaching Young Children in Violent Times

BUILDING A PEACEABLE CLASSROOM

second edition

by Diane E. Levin, Ph.D.

With Foreword by James Garbarino, Ph.D.

EDUCATORS FOR SOCIAL RESPONSIBILITY

naeyc

NATIONAL ASSOCIATION FOR THE EDUCATION OF YOUNG CHILDREN

Contents

Preventing Violence Is Everyone's Business

When my son was 17 we lived on the South Side of Chicago. Our neighborhood bordered some of the city's worst "war zones," the neighborhoods where community and family violence was endemic. Nonetheless, my son felt rather safe by virtue of his middle-class and Anglo position. The daily newspapers and television news affirmed his privileged status: rarely were a white face and an Anglo name to be found among the victims of lethal violence. That was 1993.

Fast-forward to 1998. We now lived in Ithaca, New York, a lovely university town in the Finger Lakes Region. People come here to avoid the dangers of big city life. The morning after the school shootings in Jonesboro, Arkansas, in 1998, my 16 year-old daughter sat at the breakfast table reading the newspaper. After she finished the detailed account of the attack by 13 year-old Mitchell Johnson and 11 year-old Andrew Golden on their school mates, in which four people were killed, she looked up and said, "I wonder who it will be in our school?" Her newfound sense of vulnerability is shared by children and youth everywhere— by parents, teachers, and administrators throughout the country. This shared sense can become a positive source of motivation to do something constructive or a paralyzing fear that drives us to unwise and nasty punitive strategies. This book represents the positive face of our shared vulnerability.

For the past 25 years I have been studying the problem of violence in the lives of children, youth, and families, in homes, in schools, in communities, and in war zones around the world. Most recently I have been interviewing boys incarcerated for committing crimes of lethal violence, both as a researcher and as expert witness in youth homicide trials. My work focuses on boys, who commit more than 90% of all lethal assaults and who are the predominant perpetrators of non-lethal assault as well, but applies to all children.

Over the past 25 years there has been a doubling of the percentage of children and youth who have mental health and developmental adjustment problems severe and chronic enough to warrant professional intervention, according to the research of psychologist Tom Achenbach.

The spreading problem of youth violence is related to this larger development. Dealing with it will require both a broadly-based prevention perspective on community life as well as a conscious focus on dealing humanely and effectively with troubled aggressive children lest they fall in line with the downward spiralling pathway to youth violence.

There are many reasons why kids turn violent, but there are also many ways parents and professionals can work to reverse violent tendencies in youth and thus make schools and communities safer. No matter how effective, motivated, and attentive any of us is as a parent, our children go to school with kids who are lost and who have access to weapons. There are kids in every school who have developed a pattern of aggressive behavior, who have established an internal state in which they see themselves as victimized by peers and society, and whose emotions and moral judgements have been harnessed to their aggressive rage, which can in turn lead to violence.

The problem of youth violence usually starts from a combination of early difficulties in relationships that may arise from a child's difficult "temperament" and the pattern of escalating conflict that develops as a response to such "temperament." These patterns of response increase the odds that these vulnerable children will become increasingly frustrated and out of sync as they react to their pain by not paying attention in school and beyond. Troubled kids will be as bad as the social environment around them. I have identified this as the issue of "social toxicity," the presence of social and cultural "poisons" in the world of children and youth. The glorification of violence on television, in the movies, and in video games is part of this social toxicity, and it affects aggressive kids more than others. Just as asthmatic children are most affected by air pollution, so "psychologically asthmatic" children are most affected by social toxicity.

Teachers and parents, however, play a crucial role in overturning this cycle of aggressive and anti-social behavior. Moreover, research by Sheppard Kelam and his colleagues demonstrates that if the first grade classroom is well organized and provides clear messages about behavior, aggressive kids are reclaimed and their aggressive behavior is tamed. Teachers need special skills, as Diane Levin thoroughly illustrates in her book, and a high motivation to create classroom environments that prevent violence. Knowing how these kids reach this crisis state empowers us to reduce the odds that a child will become violent. Thus, violence prevention is everyone's business. Mobilizing community leaders, parents, professionals, and kids themselves can provide a rallying point for improving the social environment.

One of the essential features of a complete program to prevent youth violence is peace education in the early childhood educational and child care settings. Young children are particularly malleable, and thus starting prevention programming early makes good scientific sense. Showing young children better ways to manage conflict is essential. Dealing with trauma—from events in the home, the neighborhood, and the larger society—is critical. Modeling non-violent conflict resolution is important. Replacing shameful "isms" with enlightened acceptance is fundamental.

This is where this book comes in. *Teaching Young Children in Violent Times: Building a Peaceable Classroom* is an essential tool for the early childhood educator who wants to make a positive contribution to peace and violence prevention in our society. It serves as a toolbox for translating good intentions into effective classroom management and teaching practice. I always ask my students to embrace as a central principle of intervention the saying, "you can change the world...but unless you know what you are doing, please don't." This book helps each of us who cares about young children and the quality of life in our society to heed that message. It allows us to address the problems, understand their roots, develop alternatives, and work together to know what we are doing and thus how to change the world for the better.

James Garbarino, Ph.D.
Co-Director, Family Life Development Center
Elizabeth Lee Vincent Professor,
Human Development,
Cornell University

From Turtles to Doves:
The Challenges of Teaching Children in Violent Times

The Need for Peaceable Classrooms in a September 12th World

At noon on September 11th, I received a phone call from the Dean of Education at Wheelock College where I am on the faculty. Wheelock student teachers, who had begun working at their placements the day before, would be at the college on September 12th for their first weekly seminar of the semester. As a faculty member who had done a lot of work in the area of children and violence, I was asked to meet with the students to help them process their experiences at their placements in light of the tragedy that had just occurred.

I hung up the phone feeling relief at having found something concrete I could do to help others help children deal with what had just happened in the world. My sense of relief was quickly replaced by a new reality—the magnitude of the tragedy of September 11th. While many children around the world have grown up and continue to grow up with violence that is hard for most of us in the U.S. to imagine, at first glance, what happened here on September 11th seemed unlike anything that had ever happened before. Would anything I had written about children and violence in the past provide guidance for dealing with the present situation?

I decided to start the discussion with student teachers using the same approach I have always used when discussing any traumatic and difficult situation—by collecting information about what happened at the students' schools and in their classrooms. What did they find out about what the children already knew and understood? Was there evidence that children were feeling their own sense of safety threatened? What questions were the children asking through their words and actions? And, finally, what questions, feelings, and needs did the graduate students themselves have as a result of their experiences with the children? The answers to these questions would provide the information I needed to figure out how children's responses and needs in the current crisis were similar to and different from the children's past experience with violence. They would also provide a foundation on which to help students build an understanding of children's needs and to develop possible response strategies.

When I met with the students, they already had a lot of information and experience from their placements that they wanted to share, as well as many feelings, questions, and concerns that they needed help working through. They described the wide range of children's responses to what they had seen and heard about the tragedy. Some knew a great deal about what had happened while others seemed to know very little. Some spent the evening watching TV news with their parents, while others had been shielded from exposure to the photographic images. Some wanted to talk about it a lot, while others didn't seem to have much interest in discussing it at all. What children seemed to understand or be confused about varied considerably, as did the degree to which they expressed anxiety and concern.

Some children brought content from September 11th into their art (tall buildings on fire) and into their play (block towers getting knocked down by airplanes and children burying themselves under piles of blocks). There were older children who wrote and illustrated stories about how their families were worried about relatives who lived in New York City, about parents who flew in airplanes a lot, and about a mother who worked in a skyscraper in Boston.

Students also described a wide range of adult and school responses. For instance, most adults had an immediate and ongoing need to talk about their own reactions to what had happened on September 11th with other adults. Taking care of one's own needs around issues of violence is an important prerequisite for being available to help children meet theirs. In addition, parents and teachers alike were struggling over how much to tell children and how to respond to the questions children asked. Many wanted to protect children from the news and hide the reality of the horror, while others believed children would inevitably hear about it and wanted this to happen in a "safe" environment with trusted adults.

Most schools recognized that the magnitude of September 11th required some sort of school-wide response and therefore quickly went into action. Many sent letters home to parents about how the school was responding and offered advice about what parents could do and talk about with their children. Some principals and center directors sent memos to teachers with instructions about how to handle the situation, which ranged from suggested guidelines for talking with children to decrees that teachers could not talk to children at all about what had happened. There were emergency assemblies to tell the children about the events, and at the end of the day, staff meetings were held to develop a plan for September 12th. There were also announcements over school public address systems informing children of what had occurred. Some schools even turned on television sets so children and teachers could watch. Some parents began arriving at schools that morning to pick up their children. A few schools decided to close early and called parents to come and get their children.

As Wheelock student teachers recounted their experiences, we heard about the impressive array of thoughtful and seemingly appropriate response strategies that were put into practice at their schools. But often, the initial response turned out to be the start of a more complicated, less predictable process. In one elementary school, for instance, letters to parents on how to talk with their children about the tragedy were put in cubbies without any discussion with the children about what had happened. To the discomfort of one second-grade teacher, children started reading the letters (which were not in envelopes) as they took them from their cubbies and began asking her questions to which she felt compelled to respond. Despite the school's decision to have parents break the news to their children with the help of the letter, this teacher felt a responsibility to sit the children down then and there to discuss what they had read.

The teacher in one kindergarten carefully planned to have a discussion with her children when they arrived on September 12th, only to find she became teary-eyed near the end of the discussion. While feeling uncomfortable about how her tears might affect the class, the children took it as an opportunity to talk about times they felt sad and cried and what had helped them feel better.

And at one preschool, the director collected information from parents when they brought their children to school on September 12th about what the children did and did not know concerning the 11th. Then, in order to protect children and respect parents' wishes, she instructed teachers to base their conversations with individual children on what each individual child already knew. Soon after arriving at school, several children who knew what happened went into the block area and began building towers and using toy airplanes to loudly knock them down. The teacher wanted to talk to them about what they were doing. But she faced a dilemma about how to respect the school's policy as children who did not know about the events ran over to join the action and the builders excitedly proclaimed, "Some planes crashed into buildings, and the buildings fell down just like in the movies!"

I learned a great deal on September 12th that confirmed, but also supplemented, what I already knew about children and violence. In the weeks and months that followed, I learned more as children struggled to sort out what they had heard about the post-September 11th world—with heightened levels of security, fear, and events such as wars with Afghanistan and Iraq.

Many children are exposed to more violence now than ever before. Even very young children see news violence on a scale I had never imagined possible. They use what they have learned from prior experiences with real and entertainment violence to try to make sense of their new exposures to violence in their own unique ways. Now more than ever they need help from adults in dealing with the violence that surrounds them.

I was very encouraged that in the days following September 11th, adults were finally taking the needs of children in violent times seriously to a degree that I had never seen before. They were devoting more time, thought, and resources to trying to meet those needs. Many of the adult responses I heard about illustrated the best of Peaceable Classroom[1] practice.

At the same time, with each new effort, I learned more about how children make sense of what they hear and what they need as a result. No matter how well thought out a particular response strategy was, it only provided a starting point, because the responses it generated were rarely predictable and often moved in unexpected directions. There were few foolproof recipes for what to do. Effective responses worked best when they were seen as part of an ongoing process that evolved and grew in ways that took into account the responses and needs of individual children as well as the whole group.

Learning from the Past

The rapid mobilization that occurred to help children deal with the aftermath of September 11th, 2001 quickly slowed down in most schools as the more overt signs of impact on children began to diminish. Many adults breathed a sigh of relief that they would no longer need to deal with the disturbing issue of violence with their children. But for me, the lessons I learned on that day made me realize that it was time to begin work on the second edition of this book.

I was reassured that the basic principles, strategies, and underlying assumptions of a Peaceable Classroom, as described in the first edition of *Teaching Young Children in Violent Times*—especially its focus on a developmental approach—are still at the core of what children need today. I wrote the book in 1993-1994 because I was hearing in my work with teachers and parents about the many ways violence was entering the lives of children from all walks of life. There was a lot of talk about angry and aggressive children who were hurting themselves and others. Teachers said they were not adequately prepared to understand or deal with these children and could not find adequate resources to assist them.

Then, there were the painful stories I heard about children who were experiencing real-world violence: a preschooler involved in a serious automobile accident caused by a speeding drunk driver; a five-year-old whose teenage sister committed suicide with a gun; a child who saw a homeless person bleeding from a stab wound one morning on the way to his child care center; a boy who saw his father stab his mother and then be arrested by police.

In addition, at a time when the media was playing an increasing role in children's lives, there was

---

[1]Others have used the idea of a Peaceable Classroom. For instance, see W.J. Kreidler, *Elementary Perspectives: Teaching Concepts of Peace and Conflict*, (Cambridge, MA: Educators for Social Responsibility, 1990).

also a rapid escalation in the violence in children's media and in the violent toys and other products that were marketed to children through TV programs and movies. We had already experienced the Teenage Mutant Ninja Turtle[2] phenomeon in 1994. The Mighty Morphin Power Rangers craze had just begun and was discussed in a hurriedly-written appendix as the book was going to press.

Teachers were voicing increasing concern about how they saw this violent media culture influencing the behavior and play of the children in their classrooms. I often heard groans from teachers when I would mention the Teenage Mutant Ninja Turtles. I heard about children who did not know how to resolve their differences without resorting to fists, and others who were obsessed with imitating the actions of the Ninja Turtles in their play.

Through this work, it became all too clear that the many forms of violence in society that were entering the lives of young children were affecting the very foundation these children were building for understanding how people should treat one another and resolve their problems. Meanwhile, teachers were asking for help as to how to counteract the harmful effects they felt the violence was inflicting on children and on everyday classroom life.

Many conflict resolution programs had sprung up around the country in response to increasing aggression and violence among children in their homes, schools, and communities. But most of the programs were for children in upper elementary grades through high school, not for children under eight years old. Perhaps this is because as children get older their failure to learn positive social skills causes more problems for adults and becomes potentially more dangerous to others. It may also be that because of how older children think and learn, it often seems easier to teach them specific behavioral skills through direct instruction and discussion.

For whatever combination of reasons, the specific needs of younger children in the face of violence in society were largely ignored in 1994. We knew that early experience influenced behavior and development. We knew that children did not start learning about peace and conflict in the middle years and that young children were being affected by the violence in their lives. We also knew that the foundation for understanding how people should treat each other and deal with their conflicts is laid in the early years.[3] Yet few adults had adequate, if any, preparation for dealing with the effects on children of increased violence in society, much less for teaching children how to live with others.

When I wrote the first edition of *Teaching Young Children in Violent Times*, one of my major goals was to convince educators and parents that in the violent times of the 1994 world, young children desparately needed our assistance in dealing with the violence to which they were being exposed. I hoped the book would help increase awareness of the importance of confronting the effects of violence in our work with children and make it a legitimate part of the agenda of early childhood educators. I hoped to provide the kind of background information and practical strategies that equipped teachers and parents to meet children's diverse needs in violent times and to counteract the harmful lessons about violence that children were learning. My underlying approach was to offer information that was prescriptive enough to provide concrete strategies that could be readily applied in classrooms, while at the same time flexible enough to adapt to the complex and individual needs of children and the changing circumstances in society.

It has been nearly a decade since the first edition of this book was published and I have seen encouraging signs that the issues that led to my writing the book—both within schools and in our society in general—have begun to be seriously addressed. More attention is being paid to the needs of

---

[2]A new and updated version of the Teenage Mutant Ninja Turtle TV program with related products was introduced by Fox TV in the winter of 2003. Not surprisingly, it is reported to be a darker and more violent version than the original.

[3]Researchers have now concluded that a child's aggressive behavior at age eight is highly predictive of aggressive behavior in adulthood; for instance, see: L. Eron and R. Slaby, "Introduction" in *Reason to Hope: A Psychological Perspective on Youth and Violence*, eds. L. Eron, J. Gentry, and P. Schlegel (Washington, DC: American Psychological Association, 1994).

young children in violent times. Violence prevention programs are being developed for early childhood settings. More opportunities exist for teachers to receive training on dealing with the violence in children's lives.[4]

In addition, in my own work, I have seen growing interest among parents and teachers to violence and Peaceable Classroom issues. Those who have used the book said that it gave them a framework and the tools they needed to feel more empowered working with children in violent times. Furthermore, the importance of working on this topic with children has been increasingly recognized in the early childhood community. This shift in thinking is exemplified by the growing number of resources on young children and violence as well as by the welcomed decision of the National Association for the Education of Young Children to co-publish the second edition of this book with the original publisher, Educators for Social Responsibility.

Looking to the Future

With September 11th, the talk in the news about fighting terrorism, and the war with Iraq, has come an enormous new challenge for meeting children's needs in violent times. But even as news violence takes on greater importance, there is still much work to be done in dealing with the other ways violence enters children's lives. All of this violence contributes to the lessons children learn about how the world works and how people treat each other, thus greatly influencing what kind of members of society today's children will become.

At the same time, I realized how much more we have learned about violence and children since 1994 that has helped us respond effectively to children's needs in the wake of September 11th. For instance, we now know more about risk factors and how they contribute to the impact violence has on children as well as the factors that build resilience in children against the harm caused by violence. There is more research information and resource materials available to assist us in our efforts. There is also much more readiness among educators and parents to take on the task of meeting children's needs in violent times.

Moreover, teachers, parents, and students themselves have continued to teach me a great deal about working with children on issues of violence. I am especially excited about what I have learned from those who have used the ideas in the first edition of the book and have shared a wide range of original and meaningful examples of how they took the ideas and extended them. I have incorporated many of these examples into this new edition, including two new chapters: one on helping children deal with what they hear in the news and the other on writing conflict stories with children.

Children growing up today need Peaceable Classrooms now more than ever. They are exposed to increasing levels of violence in their personal lives and through news and entertainment media. Learning how to meet children's needs in violent times is still an enormous challenge for us all and is unlikely to dissipate anytime soon. Nothing can substitute the need to change the factors in society that are bombarding young children with violence, undermining their development of positive social skills, and contributing to the violence that results from—and perpetuates—social and economic injustice. In today's world, those who are concerned about the wellbeing of children have no choice but to use the best information and resources we have to help children deal with the violence they see and then to help them learn nonviolent alternatives.

---

[4]However, the growing pressure being placed on the early childhood community to emphasize early literacy instruction and testing of skill acquisition threatens to undermine many of the gains we have made promoting violence prevention in early childhood classrooms.

Assumptions that Guide this Book

This book aims to help you in your daily efforts to teach children how to live peacefully in today's world. It grows out of several basic assumptions about young children and how they can best learn to cultivate peace and conflict resolution in violent times.

Prevention and Intervention Go Hand in Hand

Efforts to break the cycle of violence have to focus as much on prevention (i.e., teaching young children how to live peacefully) as on intervention (i.e., helping children make sense of and work through the violence in their lives). On a daily basis, children are taught that violence is an appropriate response to conflict in the world around them. To reduce the negative effects of violence, we need to place lessons about peace and conflict resolution at the heart of our daily work. Toward this end, this book is organized around the idea of creating Peaceable Classrooms with young children. A Peaceable Classroom is a place where children learn how to live together in a respectful and empowering classroom community. It involves infusing trust and safety, responsibility, mutual respect, and cooperation into all aspects of the classroom.

The Roots of Global and Democratic Education

Peaceable Classrooms provide the best foundation for helping children become participants in a democratic and global community. How young children learn to treat others becomes the cornerstone they will use for deciding how to relate to others when they are adults. Similarly, learning how to deal effectively and nonviolently with the small, concrete problems they face in their immediate world will help them develop the conceptual framework they need to find peaceful solutions to the more abstract and bigger problems they will face in the wider community in the future.

A Developmental/Constructivist Perspective

For Peaceable Classrooms to be effective, they need to take into account how young children think and learn. For this reason, I start from a developmental/constructivist perspective. We cannot just pour the ideas we want children to learn into their heads. They need to actively construct their own ideas— social, emotional, and intellectual—from their direct experience. How they do this is affected by their current level of development and the ideas they have previously developed. Children incorporate positive ideas about peace and conflict resolution into their thinking when they are first given meaningful content for building those ideas. Then they are given content that challenges and confuses the ideas they have learned about violence and aggression.

A Holistic Approach to the Curriculum[5]

The more teachers imbue the values, goals, and skills of Peaceable Classrooms into the overall functioning and curriculum of their classrooms, the more effective and far-reaching their efforts will likely be. Thus, the principles and strategies outlined in this book promote a holistic approach to the curriculum—where basic skills, concepts, and subject areas (including conflict resolution) are not taught in isolation from one another, and where work and play flow naturally together.

---

[5]For a more detailed discussion of a holistic, integrated approach to the curriculum which discusses the important connections among social, emotional, cognitive, and academic learning in the curriculum, see *Developmentally Appropriate Practice in Early Childhood Programs, Revised Edition,* (eds.) S. Bredekamp and C. Copple (Washington, DC: National Association for the Education of Young Children, 1997).

Essential Component for Developing Academic Skills

When children do not feel safe, the energy and resources they would otherwise use to learn academic skills and content is often diverted into trying to protect themselves. Therefore, we need to recognize that building a Peaceable Classroom where children feel safe and part of a caring community is not a luxury reserved for a few or a distraction from teaching basic academic skills. Instead, it is a necessary prerequisite to effective and meaningful mastery of literacy and numeracy.

Parents as Partners

To the extent it is possible, we need to work with parents as we create Peaceable Classrooms for their children. Parents are often unfairly blamed for the violence their children bring to our classrooms. Some parents are as much victims of violence as their children are. Many more, despite their best efforts, are unable to fully protect their children from the violence that permeates society. Therefore, many parents need our support and assistance themselves. And the more bridges we can build between home and school in our Peaceable Classrooms, the greater our impact will be in promoting peaceable living for children and their families.

Peaceable Communities for Ourselves

The violence in society does not just affect children. It can also take a big toll on us as we struggle to understand and counteract the harm caused by that violence. Therefore, to be fully available to build Peaceable Classrooms with children, we all will need opportunities to safely work out our own thoughts and feelings about the violence we experience in our own lives and see around us.

A Framework for Informed Decision Making

There are few pat formulas or foolproof curriculum activities for creating Peaceable Classrooms. Every Peaceable Classroom will look different from one day to the next and from one classroom to another. Still, there are many tools and skills that can help you build a Peaceable Classroom. You will need to adapt them to the unique children in your classroom according to the content they bring through a dynamic, give-and-take process. Therefore, throughout this book, I try to provide information that will help you construct a framework for making informed decisions about establishing and developing your Peaceable Classroom.

How the Book Is Organized

The book has three parts. Part I (Chapters 1-4) provides the background information that will help you begin to build your own Peaceable Classroom. It describes the nature of the violence in young children's lives and how it affects them. It outlines how young children make sense of violence and shows how effective efforts to meet children's needs in violent times need to take these characteristics into account. It argues that to teach young children how to live peacefully, they need to directly experience the reality of living in a Peaceable Classroom community.

Part II (Chapters 5-8) provides the information you will need to put a Peaceable Classroom into practice. Each chapter explores a major aspect of learning and behavior that can be negatively impacted by violence in children's lives and also shows specific approaches you can develop in your Peaceable Classroom to counteract the potential harm caused in each area. For instance, you will see how to teach conflict resolution skills that counteract the harmful lessons violence can teach children about solving their conflicts. Strategies are outlined for helping children develop an appreciation of similarities and differences among people in the midst of all the stereotypes and prejudice that the violence they see can promote. You will learn how Peaceable Classrooms can help counteract the negative effects of media and media-linked toys on play and strategies for dealing with the violence children bring into their play. Finally, in a new chapter written for this edition, we will explore the special meanings young children make of what they hear in the news and learn a range of strategies for helping children understand the violence they encounter in the media.

Part III (Chapters 9-16) provides a wide range of practical strategies and activities to help you build your own unique Peaceable Classroom. I have included examples of how individual teachers have implemented and adapted these strategies to meet the evolving needs of the children in their settings and the changing circumstances in the world. You will see how these activities can enhance your efforts to support the development of basic literacy and numeracy skills in young children. Toward this end, there is a new chapter in this edition on writing Conflict Stories with children which grew out of the work of one teacher who developed her own way of extending the ideas and practices presented in the first edition. Part III also provides updated references and resources that will assist you in your efforts.

A Note of Realism

I need to warn you (as if you did not already know!) that your efforts to create a Peaceable Classroom will not be easy. Those who care for children cannot single-handedly solve all the problems that violence creates in the lives of children, families, schools, or the wider society. There are complex, difficult, and often frightening issues involved in this work. Your efforts will often be ground-breaking and sometimes controversial. There will not always be obvious solutions to the problems that arise. You will be striving to create a classroom that looks very different from the ones you inhabited when you were in school, and for many of you, very different from the kind of classroom you were taught to create! In addition, you, the parents, and children with whom you work will have very different levels of comfort, experience, and skill working together towards accomplishing the goals of Peaceable Classrooms.

So try not to change too much too soon. Start where you feel most confident and build slowly from there. Expect failures and try to learn from them. See your efforts as part of the process of working toward a goal. Team up with colleagues and other professionals with similar interests and concerns, so you can help and support each other's efforts.[6] And remember that while you will almost always feel like there is more you could and should do, your efforts will make a difference in the lives of the children with whom you work.

Finally, I feel compelled to acknowledge that it is not fair to place so much of the burden of coping with violence in society on children, parents, or teachers. Creating a Peaceable Classroom is not the solution to that violence. Ultimately, it should be society's responsibility to create an environment that supports parents' and educators' efforts to raise healthy children. But, given that children are growing up in these violent times, creating a Peaceable Classroom can make an important contribution to peace and nonviolence in young children's lives and in the lives of the adults they will become. Although this task may seem daunting, the prospect of what will happen to children if we do not try seems far worse.

---

[6]You can also use the contact information at the end of this book to reach me and share your successes, questions, and concerns.

Part One

Establishing a Foundation for Peace

There are a growing number of programs that provide specific lessons and activities for teaching young children the kinds of skills embedded in the Peaceable Classrooms described in this book. However, I have found that there are few foolproof formulae or recipes for creating classrooms that promote peace and nonviolence in children. Peaceable Classroom practices grow out of an understanding of how young children think; the process by which their ideas about peace, conflict, and violence emerge; and how the content from their experiences in the world influences the ideas they develop. Therefore, any effort to create a Peaceable Classroom will only be as good as the foundation teachers build for understanding these issues and practice with children.

The four chapters in Part I provide the foundation you will need to begin to create your own Peaceable Classroom. You may be familiar with parts of what is covered here from other areas of early childhood practice, but here the ideas are framed in terms of how they apply to the Peaceable Classroom. The chapters in Parts II and III can be read and be helpful as stand-alone chapters. However, the more familiar you are with the content in Part I, the more you will be able take the ideas in Parts II and III and transform them into practices that evolve with and are uniquely meaningful and relevant for your children.

1

Growing Up in a Violent World

A childcare teacher takes a few of his preschool children on a shopping trip to buy food for a cooking project. At the checkout counter one child runs up to the teacher, grabs his leg, and starts to cry. The teacher sees a police officer coming into the store. He realizes that police officers came to the child's home and arrested his father for armed robbery two days before.

The day after September 11th, 2001, a group of children in an afterschool child care program are building towers and knocking them down. One child says excitedly to the others, "Did you see those buildings fall down? It looked just like *Independence Day*! I saw it this summer."

A seven-year-old child kills his three-year-old brother using a professional wrestling move he saw a wrestler use on television. When questionned by police he begins to cry and says he didn't mean to hurt his brother. He was just horsing around with "pretend" wrestling moves.[1]

A six-year-old boy gets angry at a girl on the playground and threatens to get a gun and shoot her. The teachers appropriately help the children work out the problem. The next day the police come to the program director and ask to see the school's "Zero Tolerance Policy Statement" required of all schools in their community. It turns out the girl told her parents about the boy's threat when she went home and they called the police. This event happened soon after the six-year-old boy in Flint, Michigan shot and killed his classmate with his uncle's gun.

The Violence in Children's Lives

From a very young age, many children growing up today experience a great deal of violence. While the amount, severity, and degree to which they are affected vary across society, few children are exempt. In fact, the level of violence in children's lives has led clinicians and policymakers to label it a serious public health problem. Researchers have concluded that violence is a learned behavior and that patterns of aggression at age eight are highly correlated with levels of aggression in adulthood.[2] This points to the importance of our efforts to promote violence prevention when children are young.[3]

The accounts above graphically illustrate how violence does not just wash over young children. Rather, children struggle to make sense of what they see and hear in their own, often unpredictable and unique, ways. As they do, they are building ideas about how people use violence to solve their problems and also about how they themselves should act. At the same time, they may not be learning what they

---

[1] Associated Press – Reuters story in the *Toronto Star*, July 3, 1999.

[2] Eron, L. and Slaby, R., "Introduction," in *Reason to Hope: A Psychological Perspective on Violence and Youth*, eds. L. Enron, J. Gentry, and P. Schlegel (Washington, DC: American Psychological Association, 1994), 1-22.

[3] As we work to do this, it is essential to keep in mind that the causes of violence in society are deeply connected to social and economic injustice, indifference, and neglect. While beyond the scope of this book, these issues must be addressed as part of dealing with the problem of violence for deep and lasting change to occur.

need to know about how to interact with others in positive social ways that do not involve fighting.

Adults who have experienced or read accounts like those above are often surprised, even shocked, to learn that children as young as four, five, and six years old are thinking about violence. When children do bring up such issues, we are often caught off-guard and feel uncertain about how to respond. Few parents or professionals have received the guidance they need to help young children deal with the violence in their lives.

All American children and youth pay a high price for the direct violence that surrounds them. Too many of society's resources that could go into supporting children's healthy development are now diverted into combating the effects of violence. Violence is the second leading cause of death for young people.[4] More than 10 children and teenagers are killed with guns every day.[5] The homicide rate for 15- to 24-year-olds is higher than the homicide rate of 11 industrialized nations combined.[6] The Children's Defense Fund reports that over 2500 children in public schools are corporally punished every day, and in 1998, there were an estimated 2.9 million cases of suspected child abuse and neglect. Young children are most at risk for being abused and neglected.[7] And it is estimated that between 3.3 million and 10 million children witness violence in their homes each year—ranging from hitting, punching, or slapping to attacks with guns or knives—and that these children tend to be more aggressive and have more behavior problems.[8]

Whether or not children encounter violence primarily from direct experience, they have ample opportunity to be exposed through the news media. Increasingly, news media focuses on showing the horrendous things people do to each other, thereby sending the message that adults solve their problems with violence. While children cannot fully understand the nature and meaning of what is going on, many regularly see world leaders, governments, and terrorists resolving their conflicts through violence.

We also need to look at the impact of the unrelenting entertainment and fantasy violence in the media that gives children daily doses of pretend danger, war, and fighting that are depicted as glamorous, exciting, and fun. The quantity and realism of violence created for children has continued to escalate since 1984, when children's television was deregulated by the Federal Communications Commission. Deregulation led to program-length commercials—programs developed to sell children highly realistic toys that replicate the characters and props on the show as well as many other products with the logo from the program, from tee shirts and lunch boxes to bed sheets and breakfast cereals. There has also been a steady escalation of media cross feeding whereby TV programs are used to promote movies that in turn promote video games.

The use of media to market to children has been enormously successful and changed the face of childhood culture. Within one year of deregulation, nine of the ten best-selling toys had TV shows. And the most successful shows were violent: one of the most popular, "Transformers," had 83 violent acts per hour. Other highly popular programs since deregulation include: "Masters of the Universe," "GI Joe" (which has had a new TV program and line of toys introduced since September 11th, 2001), "Teenage Mutant Ninja Turtles," "Power Rangers" (still popular as it began its second decade on the air in 2003), and more recently, "Pokemon." All of these shows have a similar underlying plot—bad guys attack good guys for reasons that are hard for young children to understand. The good guys can do whatever they want because they are good, and they always win; but they can never relax and feel safe, because the bad guys always come back to attack again. And most recently, we have the highly popular "World Wrestling Entertainment" (WWE), which has succeeded as a phenomenon popular not just with children but with teenagers and adults as well.

[4]Snyder, H. and Sickmund, M. *Juvenile Offenders and Victims: 1999 National Report.* (Washington, DC: Office of Juvenile Justice and Delinquency Prevention, 1999).

[5]Children's Defense Fund. *2001 The State of America's Children Yearbook.* (Washington, DC: 2001).

[6]Dahlberg, L., Krug, E., and Powell, K. "Firearm-related deaths in the United States and 35 other high- and middle-income countries." *International Journal of Epidemiology,* 27 (1998): 214-221.

[7]Children's Defense Fund. *2001 The State of America's Children Yearbook.* (Washington, DC: 2001).

[8]Saathoff, A. and Stoffel, E. "Community-based domestic violence services." *The Future of Children,* 9(3)(1999):98.

Young children have many opportunities to see violent media. They spend, on average, six and a half hours with media every day.[9] Children living in poverty and urban areas watch an average of 50% more.[10] On television alone, children will see over 8,000 murders and 100,000 other acts of violence by the time they finish elementary school, including 20-25 acts of violence per hour during commercial programming designated for children (versus five to six acts per hour on prime time programs).[11] And for the estimated 40% of children under age ten who have a TV set in their own bedroom, much of this viewing of violence is done without the supervision or support of an adult.[12]

These figures for TV viewing do not take into account the media violence children, especially boys, are engaged in when playing video and computer games. In recent years, the video game industry's worldwide annual sales reached $20 billion.[13] In households with children, 67% own a video game system.[14] A recent study found that nearly two thirds of a sample of E-rated (for "Everyone") games involved intentional violence, and that injuring or killing characters is rewarded or required for advancement in 60% of the games.[15]

And when children are not watching a TV screen they are often still involved with the violent images from the screen. The highly realistic toys linked to the shows encourage children to replicate the violence they have seen on the screen in their play. And the marketing of non-toy products (like bed sheets, underwear, lunch boxes, and breakfast cereals) with the logos of the shows means that children can literally go to bed and wake up with their favorite violent media heroes, who keep the violent themes, behavior, and products forever on their minds.

Today, these link-ups between violent media and toys have become an established part of childhood culture. Many of the violent toys have age recommendations for much younger than the media to which they are linked. For instance, toys linked to the World Championship Wrestling TV program, which has a rating of TV 14 (i.e., parents are strongly cautioned about the appropriateness of letting children under age 14 see the show), have been rated for children as young as three years old.

The negative impact of the violence marketed to children has been the focus of increasing concern. There is a rapidly growing body of research that shows how the violence children see in the media is harming them and contributing to the high levels of youth violence in society. In July 2000, six major medical and mental health organizations issued a joint statement about the harmful effects of viewing media violence.[16] After reviewing over 1000 studies conducted over 30 years, they concluded that the evidence points overwhelmingly to a causal connection between media violence and aggressive behavior in some children, as well as increases in aggressive attitudes, values, and behavior. Moreover, they concluded that prolonged viewing of media violence can lead to emotional desensitization toward violence in real life.

---

[9]Woodard, I., Emory, H., and Gridina, N., *Media in the Home 2000: The Fifth Annual Survey of Parents & Children.* (Washington, DC: The Annenberg Public Policy Center of the University of Pennsylvania, 2000).

[10]Rideout, V., Foehr, U., Roberts, D., and Brodie, M., *Kids and Media at the New Millennium: A Comprehensive National Analysis of Children's Media Use.* (Menlo Park, CA: Kaiser Family Foundation, 1999).

[11]Donnerstein, E., Slaby, R., and Eron, L., "The mass media and youth aggression," in *Reason to hope: A psychological perspective on violence and youth,* eds. L. Eron, J. Gentry, and P. Schlegel (Washington, DC: American Psychological Association, 1994), 219-250.

[12]Farkas, S., Johnson, J., and Duffett, A., *A Lot Easier Said Than Done: Parents Talk about Raising Children in Today's America* (New York: Public Agenda, 2002).

[13]Cohen, A. "New game [Play Station 2]" *Time* 156 (October 30, 2000): 58-60.

[14]Subrahmanyam, K., Kraut, R., Greenfield, P., and Gross, E., "New forms of electronic media," in *Handbook of Children and the Media,* eds. D.G. Singer and J.L. Singer (Thousand Oaks, CA: Sage Publications, Inc., 2001), 395-414.

[15]Thompson, K. "Violence in E-rated video games," *Journal of the American Medical Association* 286 (August 1, 2001): 591-598.

[16]American Academy of Pediatrics. *Joint Statement on the Impact of Entertainment Violence on Children.* (Congressional Public Health Summit, Washington, DC., July 26, 2000).

Figure 1.1

THE CONTINUUM OF VIOLENCE IN CHILDREN'S LIVES

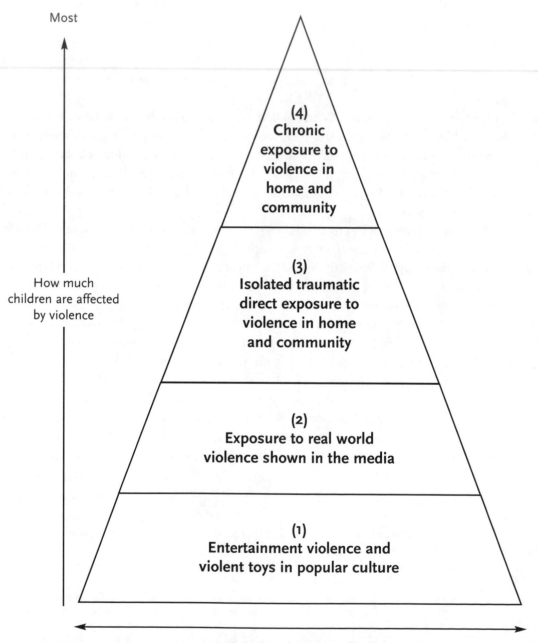

Most

How much
children are affected
by violence

(4)
**Chronic
exposure to
violence in
home and
community**

(3)
**Isolated traumatic
direct exposure to
violence in home
and community**

(2)
**Exposure to real world
violence shown in the media**

(1)
**Entertainment violence and
violent toys in popular culture**

Proportion of children affected

The Continuum of Violence Affects All Children

While children are exposed to violence in society with varying degrees of frequency and intensity, few children can escape it altogether. Each form plays a role in influencing the lessons children learn about violence and the severity of those lessons. I have found it helpful to think of the violence in children's lives as falling along a continuum, as represented on the pyramid in Figure 1.1, "The Continuum of Violence in Children's Lives."

This continuum characterizes exposure to violence as fitting along a continuum of severity. Entertainment violence (which is most prevalent in society and touches most children's lives) is at the bottom. At the top are the most extreme forms of violence—chronic and direct exposure to violence in the immediate environment (which fewer children experience but which builds on the more prevalent forms of violence below it on the pyramid). The degree to which children are affected is likely to increase as they move up the continuum, but fewer children are affected at the higher end of the continuum.[17] Children often use the content from all the levels they have been exposed to when trying to understand new content in any of the levels. This can be especially confusing when, for instance, they experience entertainment violence as fun and exciting and then experience the pain of a violent event in real life. And this can help explain why the child building the falling World Trade Center in the Block Corner after 9/11 related it to the one experience he had already had with falling towers, the *Independence Day* movie.

The issues addressed in this book will help you meet the needs of all children no matter where they fall along the violence continuum. Children at the upper end of the continuum (i.e., at the traumatic and chronic exposure violence levels) will greatly benefit from the approaches that are recommended here. However, this book does not deal directly with the special kinds of needs that exposure to violence at the upper end of the continuum creates. Therefore, most children with this level of violence in their lives will also need more help than professionals trained to work in classrooms can provide.

A Dilemma for Children (and Teachers and Parents)

Given the context for violence described above, it is disturbing to think about how the lessons young children learn about peace and conflict from their environment provide the foundation for how they will think and behave as members of the global community. The lessons society and popular culture are teaching young children stand in stark contrast to what most of the adults in children's lives value and try to teach them. It is hard not to ask ourselves, "Why does society seem to promote and glorify violence and aggression? Who benefits from perpetuating violence? Why do the needs of children and what we know promotes their healthy development so often seem to be ignored? How can a society tolerate that violence, in all its forms, is a central force in the lives of its children?"

Figuring out how to behave presents a real dilemma for children. On the one hand, children daily get media messages that say: "The world is a dangerous place, and we need weapons and fighting to keep ourselves safe." "When people have a conflict, violence is the best method for resolving it."

---

[17] This continuum of violence provides a way of looking at what researchers often call "risk factors." Risk factors are those aspects of children's lives that undermine their healthy development such as poverty and racism. Violence and media violence has also been identified as a risk factor in children. The more risk factors that accumulate in a child's life, the more that child is at risk for becoming violent. From this perspective, the further up the pyramid continuum a child's exposure to violence falls, the more risk factors are in that child's life. Researchers also describe factors that build "resilience" in children, the ability to resist the harmful influences that violence and other risk factors can have on behavior and development. It is my hope that this book will help you build the kind of resilience in children that will help them to resist the negative impact of risk factors related to violence. For more information see: *Violence and Youth: Psychology's Response. Vol. I: Summary of the APA commission on Youth and Violence* from the American Psychological Association (Washington, DC, 1993) and *Lost Boys* by J. Garbarino, (New York: Grosset/Putnam, 1999).

"Fighting is normal, acceptable, and fun." "People are either all good or all bad." "Bad guys are bad because they look different." "If you are good, it's okay to be violent in order to get what you want." "In every conflict, there's always a winner (the good guy) and a loser (the bad guy)."

On the other hand, children regularly hear adults say: "Don't hit. You need to use your words." "It's not okay to hit to get that toy. You need to take turns." "That toy is for everyone to use. If you can't share it, you will have to use something else (or go to 'time out')." These messages tell children to treat others respectfully and resolve their conflicts without violence.

But it is expecting a lot of children to ask them to choose our nonviolent approaches over the violent messages they are hearing all around them in the mass culture. Where are they supposed to learn "the words to use" to solve their problems without violence when so much of what they hear around conflict resolution is violence? As will be discussed in Chapter 3, young children do not have the cognitive skills to sort out these two divergent messages on their own. Our messages of nonviolence can seem quite impotent and dull next to the power, and often glamour, associated with the violence they see in the wider world.

Then, when children try using the violence that they see in their play and in conflicts with others—as is the normal approach children use to make sense of experience—adults often end up blaming and punishing them when other children get hurt. For instance, we are seeing more "zero tolerance" policies, like the one mentioned by the childcare director at the beginning of this chapter, that are leading to such responses as more and more children are getting expelled from school at younger and younger ages. These approaches fail to take into account the developmental understanding or needs of young children and do nothing to teach them nonviolent, alternative ways to solve their problems.[18]

To learn to be a responsible member of a caring and peaceful community, where everyone is treated with respect, children need many opportunities to build a repertoire of positive social behaviors, attitudes, and skills (see Chapter 2 for a discussion on how children construct that knowledge). As mass culture provides more and more models of violent and other antisocial behavior, and fewer positive alternatives to violence, young children are denied information that could help them build the repertoire of behavior and skills they need to behave nonviolently. And, as children spend more and more time watching television and playing video games and less time playing creatively and nonviolently with toys and other children, they have fewer chances to try out and develop a range of positive ways to interact with others and be constructive members of a social community.

Finding a New Approach

Today, many seasoned early childhood teachers report they are finding more young children arriving in group settings with fewer skills for interacting constructively with each other than they had in the past. They are seeing more children use anti-social behavior, such as hitting, verbal put-downs, and bullying[19] as a common part of their interaction with others. Often these children need a lot of help and intervention just to stay in control and not hurt themselves or others.

Yet, as will be discussed in greater depth in Chapter Five, many of the approaches commonly used in classrooms today to deal with behavior problems and aggression—like putting children into "time out" and telling them to "use your words," and now, increasingly, suspension and exclusion—

---

[18]In February, 2001, the American Bar Association took a position against "Zero Tolerance" policies in schools. The ABA argues that such policies are often unfair and inappropriate because they mandate expulsion or referral to juvenile court without regard to the circumstances of the incident or the student's history. It also argues that zero tolerance policies have become a one-size-fits-all solution to all the problems that schools confront and have defined students as criminals, with unfortunate consequences. For more information on zero tolerance (primarily with older children because few have yet addressed the special challenges zero tolerance policies create for younger children) see: *Zero Tolerance: Resisting the Drive for Punishment in Our Schools* by eds. W. Ayers, B. Dohrn, and R. Ayers (New York: The New Press, 2001).

[19]For more information on bullying see: "Bullying among Children" by J. Bullock in *Childhood Education.* (Spring 2002) 78(3):130-134.

fail to adequately address the needs created by the violence in many children's lives. These approaches assume that children have the ability to act prosocially if only they are made to do so. They also often focus primarily on restoring order to the classroom as quickly as possible so the "real" work (i.e., teaching of basic academic skills) can resume. They do not help children build the repertoire of alternative behaviors they will need to become more positive members of the classroom community now or the wider community later.

Carefully articulated and innovative approaches are needed to counteract the harmful impact violence is having on young children's healthy development and on the lessons they are learning about violence. An essential first step should be to make teaching social responsibility and nonviolent conflict resolution as valued and central a part of the early childhood curriculum as the three R's. As part of any such effort, the more you can connect what you do to parents' daily struggles to deal effectively with these issues, the more powerful and lasting an impact you are likely to have.

2

Through Children's Eyes: How Young Children Understand and Learn about Peace, Conflict, and Violence

Preschoolers Hari and Jonah, usually inseparable, are fighting over a toy fire engine they both want to play with. After much tugging and pulling, Hari roughly grabs it and runs away. Jonah bursts into tears. When a teacher comes over, he screams, "Hari's not my friend. I hate him. I'm never going to play with him again!" Hari bursts into tears.

Soon after the United States went to war in Afghanistan, five-year-old Harriet is in her family's car near an airport. Just as a plane is flying loudly overhead, the car is in a minor accident with another car. Harriet bursts into tears and gasps, "That plane dropped a bomb on us!"

Four-year-old Jama walks past a homeless person who is holding a cup, asking for "spare change." She whispers to her father, "He's bad." On questioning, Jama explains, "Well, he's dirty. It's bad to be dirty."

The father of six-year-old Ralph is about to be released from jail to rejoin the family after serving a year's sentence. Ralph's teacher tries to find out how he is feeling about this because previously Ralph has said things like, "Daddy's in jail, so he's bad." The teacher feels reassured when the discussion reveals that Ralph thinks people are bad when they are in jail and good when they are not.

A teacher overhears a group of first graders talking about the September 11th terrorist attack. One child reports, "Some people say all the terrorists on the plane died, but I know they did-n't because I heard they found one at an airport with a bomb in his shoes." Another child excitedly responds, "Maybe they [the terrorists] could jump out and get to the ground just like Spiderman, and that's how they got away."

Children Actively Construct Meaning from Experience

Children use their experience to build an understanding of the world through a slow process of construction. But they do not just passively absorb information or ideas. When they encounter something new, they actively transform it into something with unique and personal meaning, using what they have learned from prior experiences. Not surprisingly, because they do not think in the same way adults do, young children often come up with unique and unpredictable conclusions from their experience. And the conclusions they reach can deeply affect how they behave, how they feel, and what they learn.

We can see young children's meaning-making process in action in the above examples. Harriet has heard something on the news about planes carrying bombs, so when she sees and hears a plane going overhead at the same time the car accident occurs, she actively connects what she knows about planes and bombs to the car accident.

Jama may have learned at home and at school that she needs to keep clean, the way the familiar and safe people in her environment do. So when she sees a dirty homeless person, she immediately connects it to what she knows about clean and dirty. Her reaction could also be connected with a racial bias she has learned; "bad guys" are often depicted with dark skin in the media, which she may connect with being dirty.

The children's discussion about whether or not the terrorists died when the planes crashed into the buildings is an example of actively transforming new information they have heard about the plane crash into something they already understand—the special super powers that allow Spiderman to safely jump to the ground from very high places. We see the same kind of process at work in Chapter 1, when the child in the grocery store with his class reacts with fear when he sees a police officer, because the day before, the police came to his house to arrest his father.

Every Child's Ideas Are Unique

Because the meanings children construct grow out of their experiences and no two children's experiences are exactly the same, children will make different meanings, about their political and social worlds, even from the same experiences. Ralph seems to have figured out a way to understand why his father was in jail and why it is now okay for him to come home. Yet while most children may try to figure out what it means for someone to be put in jail, the fact that Ralph thinks people in jail are bad and people out of jail are good does not mean that all children at his age or level of development will think this way. Working with children to find out the unique meanings they have constructed from their experience is a vital starting point for figuring out how to respond.

The Developmental Characteristics of Young Children's Thinking Affect the Meanings They Make

While all young children's thoughts, feelings, and behaviors are unique, they are also highly influenced by the general characteristics of their age group and level of development. As you can see from the anecdotes at the beginning of this chapter, there are certain general qualities of young children's thinking that make it look quite different from mature adult thought. Seeing how the characteristics play out in children's interpretations can provide a powerful lens for understanding their needs and concerns.

- **Young children tend to think about one thing at a time.** When they have a problem with others, they have trouble thinking about more than one aspect of the problem. For instance, when Hari and Jonah both really want the fire engine, that is the only thing they can think about; their long-term friendship becomes temporarily irrelevant. Similarly, when thinking about a particular idea, young children often focus on one aspect of that idea. Harriet thinks of only one thing she knows about airplanes—they can carry bombs—not about another thing she also knows—that bombs and war are not a part of her life in her city.

- **Young children are egocentric.** They tend to interpret the world from their own point of view. When they see violence they are inclined to think about how they themselves, not others, will be affected. When they are in a conflict or feel unsafe, they usually will focus on—"What happened to me? How do I feel? What do I need to do to feel safe?" And because it is hard for young children to focus on more than one thing at a time, they often have difficulty taking points of view other than their own. We often see egocentrism at play in children's conflicts. For instance, when Hari ran away with the toy fire engine, he did not seem to consider how Jonah felt.

- **Young children often think in rigid, dichotomous categories.** They see people and things as all or nothing—all good or all bad, all right or all wrong, all friend or all enemy. Something can rarely be more than one thing at the same time. For Jonah—who thinks you can be either friends or not-friends—Hari did something bad, so he is not a friend. For Jama, clean people are good, and dirty people are bad; therefore, a dirty homeless person is bad. And for Jonah, when Hari ran away with the fire truck, he divided people into friends, who share toys, and "not" friends, who do not share.

- **Young children usually focus on the most concrete and salient aspects of experiences and ideas, not the abstract meanings or internal, less visible features or motivations.** When they have a conflict with each other, they focus on the tangible aspects of the problem, and their efforts to resolve it will usually be based more on concrete actions, materials, and physical features than on intangible thoughts, feelings, and motivations. The more salient and dramatic a concrete feature is, the more likely it is that children will focus on it. Jama focuses on the visible dirtiness of the homeless person. For Ralph, his father's location—in jail or at home—determines whether he is good or bad, not the reason that explains why he is in jail.

  Similarly, a concept like war can be easier for young children to understand than that of peace because of all the powerful and salient aspects of war that they see around them. Harriet focuses on planes carrying bombs, a tangible and dramatic part of what she has heard about war; not on distinguising between when planes do and do not carry bombs and when planes use them. Violent conflict resolution (e.g., hitting someone) can be more meaningful to the young child than the more complex and abstract process of working conflicts out nonviolently, for instance, by using words. And when children see fighting on TV, they tend to focus on the weapons and blood and guts, not on the underlying causes of the violence.

- **Young children often have a hard time seeing logical causal connections between two events.** This can make it hard for them to consider how their actions may affect others, especially in advance of performing the action. Similarly, once an event has occurred, it can be hard for young children to trace back to the behavior that led to that event. Jama does not consider why the homeless person might be dirty. Hari does not consider how grabbing the fire engine might affect Jonah.

- **Young children's thinking is static, not dynamic.** They have a hard time performing transformations in their heads—that is, they have trouble figuring out how to get from one condition to another. Thus, their thinking is more like a set of slides viewed one at a time than a movie where the movement among frames appears to be continuous. When Jonah says he hates Hari and will never play with him again, he is viewing one slide—or one moment—of his friendship with Hari. Jonah cannot imagine that a transformation could occur so that Hari and he can once again achieve a state of peace and friendship. And when Harriet thinks of the car accident, the strength of the slide with the plane going overhead overpowers her ability to see the movie of the other vehicle bumping into her car.

- **Young children's thinking often blurs the boundaries between what is pretend and what is real.** Logical thinking, including the ability to work out logical cause and effect and to make a movie about what happened, is necessary to be able to distinguish fantasy from reality. Therefore, young children's way of thinking makes it very difficult to separate the real world violence they hear about in the news from the entertainment violence they see in the media. The children connected their question about whether the terrorists in the planes that crashed into the World Trade Center actually died to their knowledge of Spiderman as they tried to figure out an answer. The children who built block towers and knocked them down referenced what they had seen in the movie, *Independence Day*. In a worst case scenario resulting in tragedy, the seven-year-old described in Chapter 1 killed his younger brother using a "pretend" professional wrestling move which presumably some adult (who clearly understood "just pretend" differently from the child) may have demonstrated too realistically but then explained as pretend. Simply telling children that violence they see on TV is "just pretend" is not a viable option to solve the problem.

Children's Ideas Change and Grow Gradually

It is rare for children's thinking to change dramatically. Rather, it goes through slow transitions from less to more mature thinking in each of the areas outlined above. Change occurs as children have many opportunities to try out their ideas, see how they work, and then modify them based on what happened. It also occurs as they have new experiences that give them new content to use in trying out and building new ideas. Thus, the process of sorting out fantasy from reality takes years of experience, as do the processes of developing logical causality or being able to take someone else's point of view. Table 2.1 summarizes the directions in which young children's thinking tends to progress along key dimensions.

Preschoolers are closer to the beginning levels of each continua. By the early elementary school, children are able to use more advanced logic to isolate concrete and familiar situations—though it is still hard for them to apply it consistently to larger, more abstract circumstances. This can lead them to continue to reach unexpected, confusing, and illogical conclusions. We see this growing (but not fully mature) logic at work when the first graders above use their newfound ability to reason about cause and effect to try to figure out how, if all the terrorist hijackers died, one survived and was later arrested at an airport with a bomb in his shoe. Their conclusions demonstrate that their thinking is still (and will continue to be for a long time) significantly different from the kinds of cognitive tasks that adults can preform.

Table 2.1
HOW CHILDREN'S THINKING PROGRESSES

FROM		TO
Focusing on one thing at a time	⟶	Bringing in and coordinating many aspects of a situation
Egocentrism and focusing on their own point of view	⟶	Being able to consider more than one point of view
Thinking in rigid and dichotomous categories	⟶	Seeing that more than one attribute defines a category and that attributes can fit along a continuum
Focusing on the concrete and visible aspects of situations and ideas	⟶	Being able to imagine what cannot be seen and to think abstractly
Failing to make logical connections between causes and effects	⟶	Making logical causal connections between events
Static thinking from one slide to the next	⟶	Dynamic thinking where transformations occur, as in the frames of a movie
Blurring of boundaries between fantasy and reality	⟶	Using logical thinking to sort out pretend from real

The children's current stage of cognitive development will affect how you can best work with them to build their understanding of peace and conflict. Because children must construct their own meanings, you cannot just expose them to more advanced thinking and expect them to adopt it. Still, there is a lot you can do to help children make new, more sophisticated meanings.

Guidelines for Practice

- **The more your efforts to promote peace and nonviolence take into account the developmental characteristics of young children's thinking and learning, the more likely it is you will teach children meaningful and lasting lessons.** Try to start from where children are along the developmental continuum.

- **The more your efforts connect to the unique meanings each child is making of his or her experience, the more likely you will be able to match what you do to the needs and abilities of the individual children in your group.** Try to start from the child's point of view and know as much as you can about experiences that have contributed to his or her unique meanings.

- **Efforts to teach about peace and conflict should point children toward what is to come.** Children's development and learning is fostered when their thinking is complicated—when they receive input that challenges and contributes to what they currently think to the point that their interest is sparked but not so much so that they cannot understand.

- **Children need an environment where they feel safe to try out their own ideas at their own level of understanding and to see how they work and where they need to be modified.** Children quickly pick up cues from adults about when it is and is not appropriate to say what they really think and know.

- **Children learn best in a supportive environment that offers many opportunities to interact with one another and to build a wide repertoire of positive ways to interact.** When they interact positively, they feel the sense of power and connectedness that so many of them sorely need.

- **Children need help getting content to use in constructing new ideas about their social and political worlds that counteracts the content provided by much of popular culture.** When bombarded over and over with powerful messages that violence and antisocial behavior are the ways to be strong and solve problems, this content will gradually be incorporated into children's understanding of how to interact with others in their world. We need to provide them with meaningful alternative content about peaceful ways to be powerful and solve problems.

- **Our efforts to help children grow up in violent times will be enhanced to the extent we are able to help parents and other caretakers learn to see the world of violence through their children's eyes, and to use this lens to develop strategies for helping their children.** Parents often feel ill-prepared to help their children work with issues of violence. You will find that many of the strategies described in this book can be readily adapted to use in the home.

From Theory to Practice

The chapters that follow focus on how to use these ideas about young children's thinking to help the children in your classroom cope with the violence that surrounds them and to learn about peace, conflict, and violence. It will help you do this in ways that take into account each individual's understandings and needs. I know teachers are often told to use child development theory in their practice, and I know first-hand that this mandate is never as easy to carry out as it sounds. Nevertheless, it is important to keep in mind it is not an all or nothing task. There is always more to learn, and there are few formulae that can apply to all situations because each situation is unique, requiring new connections and solutions.

With a topic as complex and loaded as violence and conflict in the lives of children and their classrooms, it is vital to understand and use developmental principles if we are to forge meaningful and effective ways to teach children in violent times. Yet, learning to deal with children's needs around issues of violence and conflict poses a new challenge for many of us, so figuring out how to put theory into practice poses special challenges. In some cases, it may even require coming up with totally new ways of thinking about development and teaching.

At the same time, I have always felt a kind of purposefulness and power that few other aspects of my teaching can match when I have figured out how to translate developmental theory into practice (and vice versa). Using theory has helped me to solve problems and make decisions about practice that connect deeply to children and truly meet their needs. It has given me a way to look honestly and openly at the effectiveness of my teaching, providing a constructive rationale for explaining and justifying to others what I actually do in my teaching. Moreover, it has helped to keep my work with children and adults endlessly interesting and satisfying through all of these years. This has convinced me that it is well worth the effort.

3

Setting the Stage:
The Peaceable Classroom

Because young children learn best by doing, learning about peace, nonviolence, and conflict resolution needs to grow out of directly experiencing how to live as responsible and contributing members of a peaceful community—such as the Peaceable Classroom. A Peaceable Classroom teaches children, through their own concrete actions and interactions with others with the help of caring adults, what peace and nonviolent conflict resolution mean. It is a place where the teacher, while retaining responsibility for the classroom, shares power with children so that they learn from daily experience how to take responsibility for themselves and their classroom community. It is a place where teachers serve as a model for peacemaking. In such a classroom, children learn in ways that correspond to their level of development, learning style, ideas, behaviors, and skills for living together cooperatively and nonviolently. Almost all aspects of the classroom can support this kind of learning.

No doubt, the principles and practices of Peaceable Classrooms described here will match things you already do in your classroom. Others will lead you to rethink current approaches and point you in new directions. Just as children construct knowledge and skills by building on what has come before, so teachers must construct their own vision of the Peaceable Classroom, both theoretically and practically. As you read about new approaches that make sense to you, try to build them into your classroom. This gradual approach will allow you to adapt the suggestions made here in ways that suit your particular situation, style, and group of children.

What Is an Early Childhood Peaceable Classroom?

There is no pat definition of a Peaceable Classroom. There are as many ways to create effective Peaceable Classrooms for young children as there are classrooms, teachers, and groups of children. Creating one involves a dynamic, ever-evolving process. What it looks like and how it works will change from day-to-day, depending on the unique constellation of needs, interests, abilities, and experiences of each teacher and group of children as well as what's happening outside the classroom.

A Class Discussion about Safety

The group meeting below illustrates how one teacher incorporated key features of Peaceable Classrooms into daily classroom life. This discussion with kindergartners grew out of the unique issues and needs of one particular group of children. It took place at an end-of-the-day class meeting on a day when three boys had a fight over something that had become a stressful issue for the class. Before beginning the meeting, the teacher talked with these boys about her plan to discuss the issue at the class meeting to make sure it was okay with them to discuss it as a class. They were assured their names would not be used because of a class rule about not using the names of specific children at class meetings. The boys decided they felt safe talking about the problem with the whole class. The kind of discussion this experienced Peaceful Classroom teacher lead can feel pretty daunting at first glance. It is at the heart of Peaceable Classroom practice and one of the most challenging aspects to implement. The rest of the book will help you develop the understanding and skills you need to lead such discussions yourself.

TEACHER: I have been noticing something that doesn't feel safe. There are several children who make weapons when they go to the scrounge area. Then, when they're done, I've noticed that they start running around the room, pointing their weapons at other children and making shooting noises. That doesn't feel safe to me. When they do that, it makes me feel like the other children aren't safe. What do you all think about it?

HENRY: I never do that. I always make cars.

TEACHER: Yes, Henry. There are a lot of other things children can make at scrounge besides weapons. But I don't think we should talk about which children make what now. Remember, we all agreed before that it feels safer for everyone not to mention the names of specific children when we talk about problems? Right now, I want to hear how children feel when the guns are pointed at them.

WILLIAM: I hit them when they do it. That stops 'em.

TEACHER: It sounds like you don't feel safe when they point the gun at you. So then you want to hit them to try to keep yourself safe. How have other children felt when the guns were pointed at them?

MATILDA: I ran away when they came after me.

TEACHER: That's something else we sometimes do when we don't feel safe—try to get away. Anyone else?

CHARLOTTE: I don't like it. Like, how would they like it if I yelled in their face?

TEACHER: So you don't like the noises they make, either. How do they make you feel?

CHARLOTTE: I'm scared and mad.

TEACHER: So it sounds like children don't like having the guns pointed at them or the noise they make. And some of you have felt like you needed to fight back and hit or run away to feel safe.

That sure doesn't feel safe to me. And you know our number one class rule: everyone needs to feel safe here. So we need to find something to do about the guns that helps everyone feel safe. When you have to hit back to feel safe, then someone else can get hurt. Then they're not safe. We've talked about that a lot before.

What are some ideas we came up with before about keeping safe that could help us now—some ways to make sure children aren't scared by weapons? I'll write your ideas down, so we can remember them all. Then we'll try to decide which ones we think we should try. [Teacher goes to a large newsprint pad on an easel.]

JULES: Use your words.

TEACHER: Okay. Any ideas about what words you could use?

JAMES: Say, "Don't hit."

MELISSA: I would say, "Go away. I don't like that."

MATILDA: You could say, "I'll tell the teacher."

WILLIAM: Say, "Go away or I'll hit you."

TEACHER: You have come up with a lot of things to say using words. [She reads through the list for the children.] What other ideas do you have about what we could do besides using words?

JUANDA: No guns at school. That's what we did at my Head Start.

TEACHER: Yes, we could say no guns made in school. Any other ideas?

MANNY: There could be no noises. I hate that.

NICK: Real guns are really, really, really loud!

TEACHER: Yes, real guns make a terribly loud noise. No one can feel safe with a sound like that. And in here I've noticed the loud gun noises seem to stop the activities other kids are doing—that's like their work time isn't safe. Any other ideas?

JOSÉ: You could only make noises outside.

TEACHER: That's another possibility.

HENRY: You could only shoot your friends.

TANAKA: I don't want my friends to shoot me.

LARRY: Only if the friend says it's okay.

TEACHER: So you could ask your friends if it's okay to pretend to shoot them? [A few children nod in agreement.] Well, you all have come up with a really good list of things to try. It's taken a long time. So let's come back to this tomorrow. Let's come back to our list and decide which ones to try. You can even try using them during the day and report back at the end-of-the-day meeting tomorrow, so we can hear how they worked. And those of you who make pretend weapons and use them in here, see what you think about how the rules work for you, too. I'll leave our list up, so you can come look at it if you need to.

While this discussion took place in a kindergarten, the general approach could be adapted for both older and younger children because children will respond based on their current level of thinking.

The Guiding Principles of Early Childhood Peaceable Classrooms

Peaceable Classrooms Promote a Sense of Trust and Safety

At the heart of an early childhood Peaceable Classroom is the goal that every child deeply feel "I Am Safe Here": my body is safe, my feelings are safe, my thoughts, ideas, and words are safe, and my work (the things I make and materials I use) is safe. With a sense of safety comes a sense of trust, one of the most basic developmental needs of children and an essential part of the foundation on which all social, emotional, and intellectual development builds. If children do not feel safe, efforts to teach them nonviolence will always be undermined. And, in these times, when the continuum of violence that surrounds more and more young children is depriving them of the opportunities they need to develop a sense of safety, early childhood classrooms must try harder than ever to provide a safe space for children.

The class meeting about safety and toy guns described above provides a poignant example of a teacher helping children learn what safety means through directly engaging them in a process of creating a Peaceable Classroom. Before the meeting, she talks with the three boys whose behavior earlier in the day led to her decision to hold a meeting. This direct communication helps them feel safe during the meeting and shows them they can work on an issue together in a nonpunitive, blame-free manner. Early in the meeting, when Henry begins to focus on things that could lead to casting blame, the teacher provides reassurance that names will not be used "so everyone feels safe." She often refers to safety in her efforts to further the children's thinking about the toy guns—whether the noises and gestures of others pointing guns feel safe, whether work time feels safe, why hitting others to deal with a problem cannot be allowed. She conveys respect for the boys' apparent deep interest in toy guns so that they feel safe sharing their thoughts about them. She also conveys through all of her words her deep care and respect for every child, a prerequisite for helping them learn to feel safe.

Guidelines for Practice

- **Help young children make a smooth and secure transition from home to school.** This is at the heart of learning to feel safe at school. Until they have established a sense of safety and trust, children put much of their energy into trying to deal with their insecurity, which can undermine your other teaching efforts.

  - Try to build bridges between home and school with familiar transition objects, such as stuffed animals and family photos.

  - Put out play materials that are likely to be part of children's prior experiences—felt-tipped markers, play dough, toy animals, baby dolls, and toy vehicles—and culturally relevant to their family backgrounds.

- Establish rituals that help children say "good-bye" to parents in the morning and "hello" at the end of the day such as putting the child's picture up on the attendance board in the morning and taking it down when it is time to go home or creating a special good-bye wave to each other at a window.

- Have a regular sequence of activities during the day, so children quickly learn the rhythms of the day and know when to expect their caretakers to return at the end of the day. In Chapter 10, Figure 10.3, "Our Daily Schedule," provides an example of one way to help make children comfortable with the day's activities.

- When possible, talk to parents or other primary caretakers in advance about special aspects of each child's family culture that can be incorporated into daily classroom life, and ask what they think will help their particular child feel safe in school.

- **Help each child learn, as quickly as possible, to rely on you to ensure her or his safety.** Young children look to adults to keep them safe. They need to know you are available, especially when they feel directly threatened. When children see you as a supportive and respectful adult they feel secure, which frees them to explore, experiment, and take risks. Moreover, you will provide a powerful model of how people in a peaceable community treat each other, which children can gradually learn to emulate.

- **Create concrete and meaningful rules, rituals, and routines that provide predictability, consistency, and order in the classroom.** This helps children feel secure because they know how both they and others are expected to behave. Like the teacher in the discussion about safety, to the extent it is possible, involve children in creating and modifying the rules. See Chapter 4 for some suggestions for rules and routines to use in Peaceable Classrooms. There are additional ideas for how to establish rules and routines in Part III of this book.

- **Teach all children what it means to keep themselves and others safe. One powerful organizing tool for this is the "Safety Rule."** A major task of the Peaceable Classroom's curriculum is helping children learn how to keep themselves and others safe. As we saw in the earlier discussion, where the Safety Rule was used to distinguish appropriate from inappropriate behavior, it can help children learn in developmentally appropriate ways about how to live safely and peacefully in a community. The teacher leading the discussion had the Safety Rule—'we need to feel safe here'—at the top of the list of class rules. When she was creating the Peaceable Classroom with her children, especially at the beginning of the year, she emphasized teaching the children how to put it into action.

  - Teach children how to keep their own and others' bodies, ideas, feelings, work, and possessions safe.

  - Help children learn to use the Safety Rule to decide on appropriate behavior for themselves and others. It can help children actively construct knowledge about living peacefully without imposing adult ways of thinking on them.

- **Let children know it is okay to bring up the ideas and experiences that are most important to them or that they are struggling to understand.** When children feel safe to say what is really on their minds, most of what they bring up will be positive and straightforward. But sometimes they may raise issues that are disturbing to us and make us feel quite uncomfortable trying to deal with them. There are numerous examples in this book of children raising such issues in their play, art, and conversations—for instance, frightening things they heard about in entertainment media, the news, or in their own lives. We often wish children did not have to think about disturbing issues, or we feel ill prepared and uncertain of the "right way" to respond. In addition, it may not be appropriate to discuss the issues raised with the entire group. However, in order to feel safe, children need to know that the important adults in their lives are there to help them sort out what is on their minds, even if we cannot always make things better.

- **Throughout the year, build bridges between the children's homes and the classroom.** The more you connect what happens in the classroom to what the children already know or care about from home, the more likely you will help them feel safe. Similarly, the more parents feel they understand and play a role in what happens in their child's classroom, the more likely they will feel the classroom is a safe place for their child.

- **Work to ensure that all of the adults involved in establishing safety for children also feel safe working with each other in their efforts.** Even though they will rarely be perfect, you need to be able to trust that your efforts to create a Peaceable Classroom and work on sometimes difficult issues will be met with respect from colleagues and parents. To achieve this goal, we need to work toward building the same kind of caring community for ourselves that we are trying to create for children.

Peaceable Classrooms Help Children Function as Autonomous and Capable Individuals

Children gradually learn to take responsibility for their actions and feel confident enough to formulate and share their thoughts and feelings. You can increase their sense of autonomy and competence by structuring opportunities for them to learn how to function as separate individuals, have a significant impact on what happens to their environment and themselves, and make a meaningful contribution to the overall life of their classrooms. Helping children feel autonomous and effectual often involves sharing with them in safe ways some of the power and control that has traditionally belonged to teachers. This does not mean giving up your role as leader; you still must maintain order, purpose, and safety in the classroom.

There are many ways you can promote a sense in children that they are important, contributing members of the classroom during class discussions like the one above on safety. Constantly ask for their ideas and acknowledge and validate each child's comment by reflecting it back to the group, writing it down on paper, considering aloud how it might work in practice, and encouraging children to put their ideas into action the next day. When a comment is made that diverts the discussion or describes unacceptable behavior (e.g., hitting), respectfully acknowledge what the child said before trying to transform the idea into something more positive.

Guidelines for Practice

- **Provide children with many opportunities to take responsibility, feel important, and make the classroom their own.** For instance, you can do the following:

  - Ask for and use the children's input on decisions about the classroom, but be prepared to give up some of your power and not always do things exactly as you would do them on your own.

  - Teach the children to help maintain the room and the materials in it. Chapter 10, Figure 10.1, "Class Cleanup Jobs," and Figure 10.4, "Helper Chart," show examples of how teachers have worked on this approach.

  - Involve them in food and snack preparation—setting and clearing tables, cooking and serving food, and washing dishes.

  - Both indoors and outside, use simple cooperative games that promote give-and-take actions and encourage children to work together for shared goals. Chapter 11 describes how to develop these kinds of "class games."

  - Help them share with classmates their contributions and accomplishments in and out of the classroom—for instance, children can share at meetings, teach others a special skill, and put things they would like others to see on a "sharing shelf."

  - Ask them their opinions and ideas when you can appropriately involve the children in making decisions about the class. Many of the give-and-take dialogues in this book illustrate teachers' efforts to involve children in the decision-making process of the class.

Peaceable Classrooms Teach Children Mutual Respect and Interdependence

A Peaceable Classroom is more than a group of autonomously functioning children who merely do not harm each other. It is better understood as a group of children who develop a sense of connectedness and mutuality with others. Learning to respect others and contribute to their well-being is not an easy task for young children. They are egocentric and only gradually learn to decenter and take into account alternative points of view. Young children also have a hard time understanding how their actions affect others or imagining what they cannot actually see.

The class meeting on safety contains many examples of how Peaceable Classrooms promote children's sense of connectedness in ways that match how they think. At the beginning of the discussion, the teacher presents the toy weapons as a problem shared by the whole group. She constantly shows the children how their ideas and actions affect others by asking them to state exactly how they experience what others do—"When they do that [pointing cardboard guns] it makes me feel like other children aren't safe. What do you all think about it?" Later, she helps children see that solving the problem requires all of them, not just the children who created the problem, to try new things. She also tries to incorporate all the children's ideas into the solution—for instance, by writing their ideas down and referring back to them later. Finally, by the very nature of the give-and-take dialogue, where multiple points of view are expressed and respected, children have many opportunities to experience the value of everyone's diverse contributions to the well-being of the group.

Guidelines for Practice

- **Help children learn to rely on each other, not just you or other adults, when they need assistance or have a problem.** Group meeting times, cleanup times, and small group project times all provide opportunities for helping children learn to rely on each other. (See "A Discussion of What You Need to Do When You Need Help" in Chapter 4 and Figure 10.4, Chapter 10.)

- **Plan developmentally appropriate activities that foster cooperation and interdependence.** For instance,

  - Instead of having an easel for one child on each side, try creating one where two children can work side by side, sharing the same paints.

  - Replace single-child swings with a tire swing that works best when three children use it together.

  - Organize cleanup tasks so children need to work in pairs or threes. (See Figure 10.1, "Class Cleanup Chart," in Chapter 10 for one example of how and Chapter 11, "Class Games: Promoting Cooperation, Perspective Taking, and a Sense of Community.")

Peaceable Classrooms Teach Children How to Live and Participate in a Democratic Community

Children's experience of how groups of people work together—for instance, distributing power and resources, making decisions, and solving problems—lays the foundation for how they will participate in groups and the wider society throughout their lives. Thus, Peaceable Classrooms create many developmentally appropriate opportunities for young children to build an understanding of the rules, rights, and responsibilities of living in a democracy. For example, through participating in shared decision making, children take the first steps towards understanding the decision-making process in a democracy.

Similarly, the group meeting created by the teacher in the "Class Discussion about Safety" models life in a democracy in a form children can best understand—having a voice in concrete decision making in the here and now, with an issue the children really care about. Except for firmly limiting hitting (which endangers children's safety and the classroom's "safety rule") the teacher does not impose her will on the children. She conveys genuine interest in the decisions they reach and creates mechanisms for a continuous process—like writing their ideas down about "words to use" so they can be referred to later and making sure children know to expect another meeting to continue their work on the problem (and solution). In these ways, she shares power with children while maintaining her vital roles as leader and authority (but not authoritarian leader). Furthermore, because the children will actually get to put their ideas into practice, the teacher provides developmentally appropriate opportunities for them to test out and modify their ideas.

Finally, this is a time when children often see violence as the method of choice for solving conflicts at home and in the wider world. Experiencing first hand how problems can be worked out safely by a group is one of the most powerful ways we can promote the values and skills necessary to believe and participate peacefully in a democracy.

Guidelines for Practice

- **Help children learn to participate in the ongoing process of developing rules and rituals and solving problems that come up in the classroom.**

  - Use small and large group problem-solving discussions as a vehicle for working on meaningful issues together.

  - Devise plans with the children for trying out their ideas and testing how they work.

  - Revisit the issue periodically to evaluate how the children's solutions are working and modify them as needed.

- **Involve children in problem solving only if you are genuinely interested in their solutions and intend to use them.** There will be issues for which you have a bottom line or that, for whatever reason, you have already decided. For instance, children's physical safety is not negotiable. While such issues are rare, be honest with children when they come up.

- **To the extent it is possible, develop similar cooperative and democratic approaches for working with adults in the school and children's homes.** Not only will this support your efforts to create a Peaceable Classroom, it can provide a valuable example for children of how the things they are learning to do now will evolve as they grow up.

Peaceable Classrooms: Now More Than Ever

Once we make a commitment to building Peaceable Classrooms, we can focus on building the approaches that work for our classrooms. Table 3.1 "Planning Violence Prevention Approaches for Young Children which Meet their Developmental Needs" provides a framework for thinking about what we need to do to meet the special challenges of working effectively with young children in violent times.

Increasingly, children experience violence, and, as a result, feel unsafe and out of control. They need help now more than ever learning how to feel safe without resorting to violence. At the same time, most early childhood teachers are struggling to cope with the effects of violence on children's feelings, needs, behavior, and ability to learn. Rightfully, they often feel overwhelmed and ill-prepared for this role.

These realities place unfair and demoralizing burdens on children and adults. Nevertheless, we cannot just close our eyes and ignore the realities. If we do, we make children feel responsible for keeping themselves safe from danger, which properly is the responsibility of the adults who care for them. One way for adults to meet that responsibility is by creating a Peaceable Classroom. As described throughout this book, Peaceable Classrooms can be an effective and deeply rewarding approach for beginning to break the cycle of violence in children's lives.

Table 3.1
PLANNING VIOLENCE PREVENTION APPROACHES FOR YOUNG CHILDREN WHICH MEET THEIR DEVELOPMENTAL NEEDS

BASIC DEVELOPMENTAL NEED	WHAT IS NEEDED TO MEET YOUNG CHILDREN'S NEEDS	HOW VIOLENCE UNDERMINES NEEDS BEING MET
To develop a sense of safety and trust	• A secure, predictable environment where they feel adults can keep them safe as they learn how to keep themselves and others safe.	• As children feel unsafe and see the world is dangerous and adults can't keep them safe, energy goes to keeping themselves safe; violence is one salient way to accomplish this.
To develop a sense of autonomy and efficacy	• Knowledge of how to take responsibility, positively affect what happens in their environment, feel powerful and important, and meet their individual needs without fighting.	• The sense of self as a separate person who can have a positive, meaningful effect on the world is undermined for many children who do not have the skills for feeling powerful and competent, getting their needs met, or solving problems without violence.
To develop a sense of mutual respect and connectedness	• Many opportunities to experience and contribute to a caring community in which people learn how to help and rely on others and to work out their problems in mutually respectful and agreeable ways.	• Their sense of mutual respect and interdependence is undermined as violence becomes a central part of the behavioral repertoire children learn about in how to treat others. Relying on others is associated with vulnerability.
To develop a positive gender identity and an appreciation of diversity	• Exposure to males, females, and diverse peoples with wide-ranging and overlapping behaviors, interests, and skills who all treat each other with respect and work out problems without violence.	• Narrowly defined and rigid gender division—where boys are violent and powerful and girls are sexy and weak—and racial, ethnic stereotyping often associated with violence undermine human development and relationships.
To work out an understanding of violent experiences	• Wide-ranging opportunities to work through and talk about issues of violence and nonviolence, as well as develop rich and meaningful art, stories, and play with open-ended play materials.	• Children have an increased need to tell their stories and construct meaning of violence in their lives through such activities as discussions, creative play, art, and storytelling.
To actively engage in personal meaning making	• Active facilitation of skills necessary to develop meanings, work through violence, and feel safe—including imagination, creativity, problem-solving ability, play and communication skills, and models for nonviolent behavior.	• It is harder for children to work through violence as tools for doing so are undermined by time and energy spent trying to cope and keep safe, time spent watching TV, and toys which promote imitation of violence.

4

Building a Peaceable Classroom through Give-and-Take Discussions

Central to any effort to create a Peaceable Classroom is teaching young children how to work together to make decisions, solve problems, and abide by decisions on how to act and treat each other in the classroom. Such discussions are also at the heart of efforts to deal with discipline and conflict resolution in Peaceable Classrooms in ways that help children feel respected and safe (see Chapter 5 on conflict resolution). One highly effective way to teach children how to live together peacefully is through give-and-take dialogues about issues that grow out of daily classroom life.[1] These dynamic discussions, with individuals or groups, teach children—in a safe way and at their developmental level—the process and skills they need to work cooperatively and solve problems with others. Here are classroom examples to illustrate how dialogues can be used. Try to think about how you might adapt them to your own needs and situations.

---

[1] For another look at how to use class meetings to solve children's problems see: *Class Meetings: Young Children Solving Problems Together* by E. Vance and P. J. Weaver (Washington, DC: National Association for the Education of Young Children, 2002).

A Discussion about Whether to Have a Regular Class "Sharing Time"

In the following example, a teacher helps kindergarten children work out whether they want a regular sharing time when children can bring up their ideas and experiences at class meetings, and, if so, how they think it should be structured. This dialogue helps the children learn to participate in group decisions and to share responsibility with their teacher for how their classroom functions. The column on the left has the actual comments made by the children and adult. The column on the right explains how what is said illustrates important aspects of Peaceable Classrooms.

CONVERSATION

TEACHER: Our question to talk about today is: "Are we going to have a sharing time?" Yesterday, someone asked: "Are we going to have sharing?" Some kids called out that they wanted it, and some kids groaned and said they didn't. So we need to figure out what we are going to do about it.

T: Raise your hand if you would like to have sharing. [Fourteen hands go up.]

T: Raise your hands if you do not want sharing. [Nine hands go up.] Now, I'm going to ask if you don't care—some kids might not care. [Six hands.]

T: So fourteen kids want sharing, nine kids don't want sharing, and it doesn't matter for six kids. Now we'll hear some reasons why you raised your hands for what you chose. First, let's hear from the kids who want sharing. Why do you want a sharing time?

COMMENTARY

The teacher involves children in deciding how they want their room to work and how they want to go about making it happen. This promotes a sense of autonomy, community, and shared responsibility.

She tells children at the outset what they will be working on. This is an effective way to begin group discussions.

She chooses a topic that comes out of a real disagreement among the children. Young children learn best from direct experience.

The teacher creates a clear structure for children to use when expressing their positions. This exemplifies a structured but open format.

She accepts the fact that twenty-nine children vote, even though there are only twenty-two children in the class. She does not impose her adult notion of one child, one vote. This supports children at their level of understanding.

She summarizes the vote but doesn't focus on who won or lost. She helps children hear each other's thinking about why they voted as they did. This models an approach to problem solving where everyone wins; fosters logical causal thinking; helps children take other points of view; and conveys that their ideas are important.

A Discussion about What to Do When You Need Help

In the give-and-take dialogue that follows, the teacher tries to show children new ways to function independently and cooperatively in the classroom.

CONVERSATION

TEACHER: I need your help. I have a bit of a problem, and since you all know me pretty well, you know the classroom, and you know each other, I thought maybe you could help me solve my problem. Would you be willing to do that?

CLASS: [enthusiastically] Yes!

T: Here's the problem. I've been noticing that sometimes in the afternoons I get really grouchy. I noticed this happens when there are a lot of kids asking me things at the same time—calling out "Teacher, teacher"—and lots of kids waiting for me to do things to help them. It doesn't feel good to be grouchy. After you all go home, I think, "Oh, I was kind of grouchy. I don't feel good about that." I was wondering if you have some ideas to help me solve this problem.

JENNA: You could let people take turns.

T: How would that work?

COMMENTARY

The teacher starts by telling everyone the issue to be discussed at the meeting.

She admits her own need/problem; this humanizes her and her role in the classroom.

She promotes the children's sense of commitment and responsibility as contributing and valuable community members.

Children clearly relish this task.

T. helps the children understand her point of view.

T. explains the problem in concrete, cause-and-effect terms.

T. does not judge children for needing help, rather she treats it as a problem they can all solve together.

Using an open-ended question, T. channels the discussion into brainstorming possible solutions—getting different ideas and points of view. She is interested in the children's ideas and does not imply there is one right answer or that she knows the answer.

A good start, but the child gives no sense of what this might mean in practice.

T. accepts answer and asks a question to help the child connect her idea to specific actions and behaviors.

JENNA: People take turns—first one, then the other.	A definite elaboration, but as is often the case with young children, it does not really solve the problem at hand.
T: So your idea is that children wait to take a turn—first, I help one child, then another, then another. Okay. Who else has an idea?	T. translates Jenna's ideas to the rest of the class but does not evaluate them. This can be a hard shift in roles for teachers, but as you'll see, it can lead to exciting results. T. keeps discussion moving and indicates she values diversity of ideas, not just right answers.
JACKSON: You could line up.	As with Jenna, he's thinking more about what children could do than how it would help the teacher's grumpiness.
T: So you could line up to wait for your turn.	She again translates for the whole group. Translating helps all the children stay involved and follow the logic of the discussion.
CARLOS: Raise your hand.	Another solution egocentrically focusing on what children do. Children often focus on variations of one kind of solution and need help going further.
T: Raise your hand and wait for the teacher—instead of calling out my name. Okay.	She keeps the brainstorming going at a good pace. Instead of judging the proposed solutions, she helps children hear each other's ideas.
RAY: Raise both hands.	Another solution that is a variation on what came before it.
ROSA: I would go to another teacher.	A possible breakthrough to a new kind of solution—i.e., Rosa might be proposing something that takes into account what can help the teacher, too.
TOSCA: Ask a child.	A transition in kinds of solutions has occurred. This one considers how both T. and children will be affected.
T: So you don't always have to go to a teacher—sometimes you could help each other? Do you mean like how you asked Kerry to help you find the tape you wanted to hear in the tape recorder?	She highlights the special cooperative nature of this solution by providing details and a concrete example of how it can work. She doesn't say it's better than the other solutions.

TOSCA: Yeah.

SAM: Oh, brother!

He feels comfortable expressing his (distressed) reaction to this approach.

T: Sam, it sounds like you don't like the idea of not going to a teacher when you need help.

T. spells out the meaning of what Sam said in an accepting, non-defensive tone. This conveys it's okay for Sam to say what he thinks, even if he disagrees (because he's not being hurtful of another's ideas).

SAM: You better go to someone who's good.

Sam seems to understand the practical implications of the children-helping-children solution.

T: Someone who's good? Can you say more about that?

She tries to get Sam to elaborate on his idea in order to help the others understand what he means.

SAM: You know. You ask someone who can do it.

T: So you think you should try to think of who's good at the thing you need help with so you can ask him or her to help you? [Several kids nod in agreement.] Who has other ideas about what we can do?

She makes explicit Sam's meaning: Children differ in how well they do various things.

The group is clearly involved with the discussion. They do not seem threatened by the idea that not all children are equally accomplished at all things.

KENDRA: Make a list.

An egocentric way to answer; she does not give enough information for others to understand her idea.

T: Can you tell us more, Kendra?

T. uses a probe question to help Kendra elaborate on her response and involve the rest of the class in her suggestion.

KENDRA: Make a list of who's good.

Tries to spell out how to make the children-helping-children solution work.

T: I think I get it. Do you mean we could make a list of who is good at what, so children who need help could figure out who to ask for help—so you would know who could help you? [There are enthusiastic nods.]	She translates Kendra's idea, making it clearer. She accepts children's premise that different children are good at different things.
T: I think a list like that could really help me not feel grumpy and it could help you all get help when you need it, too.	She assesses how this solution might affect her, again helping the children broaden their perspectives and see how the solution can meet her needs, as well as theirs.
T: We've spent a long time talking about this now. You all have sat still for a really long time. You have come up with so many good ways to help me. You have really helped me. Thank you. For now, let's stop and have snack. Tomorrow, we'll work on our helpers' list.	She decides it's time to stop because the children appear restless. She acknowledges the children's accomplishments by focusing on their positive actions (not just using praise) and does not blame them for their restlessness. She does recognize that more work is needed to put the children's solution into practice, but, rather than leave things dangling, she tells them what will happen next and when.

This discussion was the start of a long-term process in the classroom whereby children developed structures and routines for asking for help and helping each other. To find out more about what happened, see Chapter 9, Figure 9.5 "Class Graph: Did Anyone Ask You to Help Today?" and Chapter 10, Figure 10.4 "Helper Chart."

These two class dialogues, the first on sharing time and the second on how to get help, as well as the one about safety in the previous chapter, illustrate how to involve young children in classroom decision making. While the content for each discussion grew out of the here-and-now needs of the classrooms, the process of joint decision making remains a constant focus. And in each, instead of viewing solving class problems or making decisions as intrusions on the regular educational program, the teacher treats them as unique opportunities to promote learning and growth about issues of peace and conflict.

Guidelines for Practice: Leading Group Discussions

Several underlying principles used by the teachers in the above examples guide efforts to have give-and-take dialogues with young children.

- **Try to select discussion topics related to children's direct experiences and growing out of issues that have come up in the classroom.** This can help children connect what they already know to the discussion topic and see its relevance to their own behavior. It can also help assure that the issues discussed are appropriate to the diverse family backgrounds and experiences children bring to the classroom.

- **Use a structured but open discussion format.** This can help children develop their thinking about a particular issue, but it leaves room for each child to bring in his or her own unique experiences and understandings.

- **Create an atmosphere where it feels safe to express diverse ideas.** Because children have unique experiences in and out of school, they vary a great deal in their ability to participate in a discussion. Some children will feel unsafe speaking up at first. Many have learned to look for the one right answer to a question or problem and have had little experience expressing their own ideas or respecting the divergent ideas of others. The children will also have many different ideas to contribute on any topic. In an atmosphere that feels safe, where varying degrees and forms of participation are respected, they are more likely to take risks and try out their ideas with others.

- **Help children put their ideas into words and share them with others through give-and-take dialogue.** In this way, adults can help create a sense of shared responsibility and model for children positive ways to work on issues. They can also promote problem-solving skills and a sense of independence and being in control, which is especially helpful for children who have a hard time participating in discussions.

- **Establish rules and expectations for discussions.** To have successful discussions, children need to learn how to participate in a group. This can be hard for young children at first and is often best accomplished by making "discussion rules" a topic for discussion early in the year. Including children in this process (to the extent their age allows) helps them better understand the rules, and it gives them a reason to feel committed to the group's solution.

- **Ask open-ended questions with many possible answers and respect the diverse ways children respond.** Open-ended questions allow children at a wide range of developmental levels to participate comfortably in a discussion. As children learn that their unique answers will be valued and respected, they will get better at saying what they really think and feel, rather than what they think adults want to hear. At the same time, they will often need help making their ideas understandable to others.

- **Ask questions and bring in new information or ideas that complicate children's thinking.** The content you bring to discussions can be a powerful source of learning and growth. For content to be meaningful to young children, they need to be able to connect it to what they already know. At the same time, to promote the construction of new knowledge, what they hear needs to challenge their current thinking by providing a slightly more advanced perspective.

- **Find ways to affirm and validate children for whom group time and collaborative decision making may not feel comfortable or safe.** There will be a wide variation in the skill and comfort levels children bring to group discussions because styles of parenting in the home, cultural styles of communicating, and attitudes about decision making and problem solving vary among families and cultural groups. Children who have a hard time participating still need to feel respected and valued as you help them learn how to enter into the discussion. You will also need to keep the diverse backgrounds of your children in mind as you select topics for discussion.

- **When possible, end discussions with a concrete plan of action everyone can agree to try.** This can help children develop a sense of empowerment—the belief that they can do things that make a difference in their lives. And it can also help them learn that socially responsible solutions are both possible and satisfying.

- **Return to important topics from time to time to see how previous decisions are working.** Putting decisions into action, seeing how they work, and then discussing and modifying them with the aid of others can help children build new ideas and skills onto what they already know and also improve their ability to engage in a give-and-take negotiation process.

Helpful Hints for Leading Small and Large Group Discussions

Watching (or reading about) successful group discussions can create the false impression that they are easy to lead; in fact, they are not. The first year I taught kindergarten, I found running class meetings one of the hardest and most frustrating parts of many school days. When children had something to say, it was so hard for them to wait for their turn to talk. They often went off on tangents that distracted everyone from the topic at hand. They said things only they could understand. And, most upsetting to me as a new teacher, it took hard work and skill (and sometimes luck) to keep a whole class interested and involved when they could not all participate at the same time. Without such involvement, discipline problems, chaos, and a loss of the sense of safety often resulted. I found the following guidelines helped me lead a successful discussion:

- **Prepare in advance for the discussion:**
  - choose topics in advance and decide how you will introduce them to the children;
  - identify the children's likely key issues and ways of understanding the topic;
  - plan questions that will get children to express their diverse ideas and will stretch their thinking;
  - identify a variety of possible outcomes, so you can guide the children toward them, but also be ready for ideas you never anticipated.

- **Expect to make constant decisions about such issues as:**
  - what question to ask next and how to ask it;
  - how to balance the needs of individual children with the needs of the group;
  - how far afield to let comments go before bringing things back to the main topic;
  - how to pace the discussion to keep all the children interested and invested;
  - when to let "wrong" answers and values you do not want to promote go uncorrected in the service of promoting give-and-take;
  - how to incorporate new ideas and information that extend the children's thinking while acknowledging and accepting what they have to say;
  - when to end the discussion and with what group conclusions.

- **Offer children a lot of help (especially at the beginning of the year):**
  - learning how to participate in give-and-take dialogues;
  - feeling safe contributing their ideas;
  - staying task-focused in their comments;
  - filling in the words and information others need to fully understand what they are saying;
  - applying the ideas they get from the discussions to their everyday actions and experiences.

- **When more than one adult is present in your setting, plan:**
  - who will take the primary leadership role for the discussion;
  - the roles that will best facilitate the discussion—for instance, one teacher makes charts from the children's ideas while the other teacher leads the discussion, or one teacher works one-on-one with a child who is having a bad day and would do better not participating in the group discussion;
  - specific ways various adults can help children who have trouble participating in the discussion—for instance, sitting next to them or making eye contact or whispering ideas for possible contributions they could make.

Adapting Discussions to the Age and Prior Experience of Children

Here are some suggestions for adapting your dialogues to the developmental levels and needs of your particular children.

Preschool Children

The younger the children are in your class, the more you and other adults will need to:

- **Carry out discussions in smaller groups, pairs, or alone with the child.** Younger children are not developmentally ready to spend a lot of time in large groups, participating in dialogues that require a lot of listening to others when they need to be doing and talking themselves. Discussing an issue with a few children—for instance, where in the classroom to keep the scissors so they do not keep getting lost—and then briefly sharing the decision with the whole group at a more traditional circle time can keep preschool-aged children active and involved. As children gain more experience and skill talking about issues in this way, you can gradually bring these discussions to the whole group.

- **Choose simpler topics and rules, and shorter discussions that are closely connected to the children's concrete and current experience.** The topics should be relevant to the children's interests, concerns, and abilities. With younger children, who are mostly concerned about one thing at a time, something closely related to what they (and not others) are doing at the moment is often the most meaningful place to begin. Briefly working on an issue when it arises, in a way that has immediate and tangible impact, helps the children involved learn the tools and power of shared problem solving. Effective discussion topics with young children might be:

  - figuring out exactly what two children need to do and say to share a toy;
  - devising a list for who gets to take the guinea pig home each weekend; or
  - deciding whom among the children that played in the block area will put away which blocks at cleanup time.

- **Give them extra help working through issues.** The younger the children, the more difficulty they will have putting their thoughts, experiences, and feelings into words. And even when they can use words, because of young children's egocentrism, others may have trouble understanding their meaning. It is also harder for younger children to make logical connections between two pieces of information, come up with a solution to a problem on their own if they have not yet experienced it directly, or think about how their ideas might affect others. Thus, you'll need to give younger children more assistance than you would give older children. For instance, you may need to translate what a child says so it has meaning for others or suggest two possible solutions to a problem from which the children can choose. You will also need to provide more help putting decisions into action after the discussion.

Primary School Children

As children have more experience and skill and their thinking progresses, they become more able to follow and participate in the logic of a discussion. They begin to see how the various aspects of a situation connect. In other words, they become more able to make various parts of their own movies. You will find however, that while some pieces of their thinking seem to fit together in a way that makes logical sense, it is still hard for primary-age children to fit all the pieces together into a logical whole. There will still be times when their thinking seems more like that of younger children, and they will still need lots of help from adults throughout the process in the same ways described above. But you will find that over time they gradually can take more and more control over the give-and-take conversation process.

You will find that there are some primary-age children who have had few opportunities to discuss and work out ideas and problems at home or in group settings. These children's responses in conversations may seem like those of younger children. But once they are introduced to the group discussion process, many will make more rapid and extensive progress learning to participate in discussions than younger children, because the have the developmental capability of function at a higher level. In fact, you will often find that these children often get the most excited and involved in these discussions; I have always thought this is due, at least in part, to the newfound power they experience at learning how to have a positive impact on their environment. Nevertheless, at first these children will need many of the same kinds of help that are needed by younger children.

Reaching Out Beyond the Classroom

Discussion topics that grow out of children's direct experiences at home and in the classroom are usually the most relevant and appropriate ones for young children. With age, the world outside the home and classroom will play a greater role in their lives, and we have an important role to play in bringing the wider world into classroom discussions. And even with young children, there will be times when what happens in the wider community will be meaningful, and even important, to discuss.

Building Peaceable School Communities

Peaceable Schools go hand-and-hand with Peaceable Classrooms. In such schools, teachers, administrators, and parents all work together to implement at the school level the principles of Peaceable Classrooms and to support and enhance teachers in their classroom efforts. Classroom teachers will often need other adults in the school community with whom to work out personal thoughts and feelings that arise from issues in individual classrooms as well as strategies for responding to children. Parents need to know that they can go to teachers with issues and concerns about their children and vice versa. Topics will inevitably arise in classrooms on which the whole school community can and should work together.

At the beginning of the school year, for example, one kindergarten teacher had a discussion with his children about their anxiety over going out on the school playground at lunchtime (a common problem for five-year-olds entering a large elementary school for the first time). This led to a series of actions devised by the teacher and children that promoted a sense of safety and social responsibility in the whole school community. For example, during the first month of school, younger children got older children as "partners" for lunch recess, teachers assigned to lunch recess duty came to the kindergarten to meet the children before recess, and a special area on the playground was designated for kindergarten children only.

The Community Outside of School

As children hear about issues in the wider community, especially those that threaten their sense of safety and well-being, they need help making sense of what they have heard and figuring out what they can do to make themselves feel safe and even how to help others feel safe. Such efforts open up an avenue where children can talk about and work out experiences that are confusing or disturbing. Discussions of such issues can also be used to help children learn to create Peaceable Communities and to assume a role of social responsibility in the world outside class and school. All young children are working on issues of power and exploring how to affect their environment. Many have rarely felt they are important or that they can make a difference, either at home or in the community. Learning how to act on and help solve social problems outside the classroom in developmentally appropriate ways is a vital step in becoming responsible and contributing community members. Moreover, it can provide an alternative to needing violence to have an impact on the world when one grows up.

Talking about "Outside of School" Issues

When you let children initiate discussion topics on the spot, a rich array of issues are likely to come up that can enrich all children's experience. But once children feel safe raising what is important to them, it can be hard to prepare yourself adequately for every issue that will come up. Sometimes they will bring up disturbing issues they hear about in the news. (See Chapter 8 "When the World is A Dangerous Place.")

They may also bring up violence they have experienced directly in their own lives. One teacher of preschool children who experienced a lot of violence in their lives had an unexpected group discussion when Ken brought up his visit to his mother in the hospital after she had been shot. All the children knew about the shooting, so the teacher decided on the spot that they needed a chance to react, ask questions, and hear that Ken's mother was out of danger. Ken centered his comments on the beeping of the machine at the hospital (the heart monitor) that "told me my mother is okay." He had found something concrete to reassure himself (and the other children) about his mother's safety and recovery.

Ken's comments tell us what will help him deal with this distressing event—to know his mother is safe. When they have a safe place to talk, children who have experienced stress and violence often tell us what they need. This can help you figure out what role to play with a child. Ken's teacher ended this discussion by asking the children if there was anything special they could do for Ken and his mother to help them feel better, and the children enthusiastically decided to make her get-well cards that Ken could bring her on his next visit. Ken was thrilled.

When to Stop a Group Discussion

At times you will need to stop the discussion of a topic raised by a child because it is inappropriate to discuss with a large group. For instance, if Ken's class did not know about the shooting, the teacher might have decided to respectfully rechannel the discussion.

One way to do this is to acknowledge the issue when it is brought up and admit to the children that you need to think about it some more and promise to return to the topic later. Or, you might tell everyone that you need to talk further with the child who raised the issue after the meeting and will bring it back to the group later. It's important that you then make sure you follow-up on your promise.

Both these approaches are preferable to what one teacher told me she decided to do—put an end to group sharing meetings because of the unpredictable and often gruesome content children brought in.

The Roots of Social Responsibility

For many reasons, give-and-take discussions like those described here can be hard to incorporate into your classroom. Learning to lead them well is extremely challenging, and no matter how good you are, there are always places where you could do more. You are never in full control of the direction of a discussion. It takes work to help children learn how to participate fully. And it is hard to fit the discussion into already packed early childhood curricula.

Yet, when you have successful dialogues on topics that are personally meaningful to young children, you are helping them work through their experiences and ideas about peace, violence, and how people should treat each other. You are also helping them establish a foundation for living peacefully and responsibly on which they will build larger social skills and values for the rest of their lives. Learning to deal nonviolently with small problems, solve their conflicts, and affect their immediate world today will give them nonviolent ways to solve bigger problems in the wider world tomorrow. It is the heart of meaningful peace education for young children.

Part Two

Building a Peaceable Classroom

Now you can build on the foundation that was created in Part I to build your Peaceable Classroom. Each of the four chapters in Part II is designed to help you work in a positive and constructive way on a key aspect of children's learning and development that is negatively impacted by violence: teaching nonviolent conflict resolution, promoting an appreciation of similarities and differences among people, using play to promote learning and meaning making, and helping children deal with violence in the news.

Do not expect to use all the content and ideas all at once or to the same degree. How you proceed will depend on those aspects of Peaceable Classrooms you have already worked on and the specific abilities and needs of your children. No matter where you are now, it is my hope that you will find ideas and practices that empower you to take new steps toward building the kind of classroom that children need to become caring and responsible people.

5

Making Peace: Teaching Children to Resolve Conflicts Peacefully

"I find I'm spending more and more time helping my children settle disputes. Many kids seem to have fewer skills than the children I had 15 years ago when I started teaching. More kids hurt other children as soon as they can't get their way. I keep telling them to 'use words, not fists' but it's often like talking to a wall. I think some kids actually feel scared by what's going on."

Many teachers, like the one above, report concerns about levels of aggression among children in their classrooms. They say they spend too much time trying to help children feel safe, and that they often have only limited success. Some admit to resorting to more "time outs" and harsher "discipline techniques" in an effort to create classrooms where children can feel safe enough to engage in meaningful learning and play.

Part of helping children feel safe involves teaching them what they can do to keep themselves safe and how to find solutions to their problems with others that successfully meet their needs without using violence. Children gradually learn how to work out their conflicts with others, whether positively or negatively, through their experiences dealing with conflict and also by seeing how others deal with conflict. When they have aggressive or hostile experiences with conflict resolution, they learn strategies for winning conflicts by hurting others. When they have positive conflict resolution experiences, they gradually learn what to say and do to work out problems with others in a satisfying manner. It is vital that children learn these skills when they are young, because research suggests that patterns of aggression at age eight are highly predictive of later aggressive behavior. Yet today, too many children have too few opportunities to learn the content and skills they need to solve their conflicts without violence. All the violence they see in the world around them, including in the media, contributes to the problem.

This is why teaching children how to work out peacefully a whole range of needs, problems, and conflicts in varying degrees of severity is not just a necessary inconvenience in the classroom curriculum. It is at the heart of the curriculum in a Peaceable Classroom. It is one of the most powerful ways we can counteract the harmful effects of growing up in violent times and break the cycle of violence in children's lives and in society.[1]

A Discussion When Two Points of View Collide

Nathan and Delise are playing hospital in the dramatic play area of their child care center. Delise, the patient, is lying on the bed with bandages (torn strips of sheets) wrapped around her head, arms, and legs. She seems in terrible shape as the doctor, Nathan, stands over her with a stethoscope:

> **NATHAN:** [Putting the stethoscope down and picking up a play syringe] You're shot. Your heart's bleeding. You need this to get it to stop.
>
> **DELISE:** No, it's gonna hurt.
>
> **NATHAN:** Be still. You need it to save your heart. It's bleeding really, really bad.
>
> **DELISE:** [Sitting up and beginning to pull off the bandages] No! You stop that. I'm better.
>
> **NATHAN:** [Jumping up and down] Hey, wait! You're gonna die. You need this shot. [He tries to push her back down on the bed.]
>
> **DELISE:** [Pushing Nathan away] Stop that. I'm better. I'll be the doctor now.
>
> **NATHAN:** [Starting to poke her hard with the pretend "needle"] You have to get this.
>
> **DELISE:** [Reaches up, punches Nathan, and bursts into tears.]
>
> **NATHAN:** [Yelling] Teacher! Teacher! Delise hit me! She hit me!
> [A teacher and a few classmates come running over from the other side of the room.]

Delise and Nathan's cooperative hospital play has rapidly deteriorated into a fight. What started as a shared, mutually satisfying experience has become a conflict where they both feel the frustration and anger that results when two points of view collide. Not only does the conflict abruptly end their play, it also disturbs the classroom, taking the teacher and several children away from other activities.

The kind of conflict described above is typical in early childhood classrooms and could have as easily occurred twenty years ago as today. However, many teachers report that they are now spending more time dealing with such conflicts, which seem more often to lead to physical aggression and hurt children than in the past. Many children seem at a loss to resolve their conflicts in any other way.

---

[1]For a more detailed guide on teaching conflict resolution to young children see: *Before Push Comes to Shove: Building Conflict Resolution Skills to Children* by N. Carlsson-Paige and D.E. Levin (St. Paul, MN: Redleaf Press, 1998).
[2]Eron, L., Gentry, J., and Schlegel, P., *Reason to Hope: A Psychological Perspective on Violence and Youth* (Washington, DC: American Psychological Association, 1994).

Teaching "Discipline" or Conflict Resolution?

After helping the children calm down, an adult arriving on the scene might deal with this problem in one of several ways. He or she might:

- tell the children they cannot hit each other—they need to "use words" when they are upset;

- tell the children to "take turns," so that each has a chance to be both the doctor and the patient;

- put the children in "time out," where they can calm down and "think about" what happened;

- suggest a solution such as "Nathan, you have been the doctor, now it's Delise's turn" or "I'll take the 'needle' away to help you both stop being upset about it";

- tell the children to pick another activity.

Any of these approaches would probably stop the conflict—at least for the moment—and quickly return the room to normal but they present some major problems. They provide short-term solutions because they impose an adult's ideas about a solution on the children rather than significantly involving the children in finding a solution of their own. Thus, none of these approaches would help Delise and Nathan actively construct an understanding of better ways to resolve their conflicts in the future. And, none gives the children the feeling of empowerment that comes from figuring out (with the help of a teacher) positive solutions to their conflicts.

Additionally, the first three solutions do not take into account the developmental levels and abilities of these children. For instance, using "time out" and telling them to "think about what happened" assumes they have the cognitive skills to recreate on their own the sequence of events leading to the conflict and the logical causality underlying their actions. This is a tall task for young children, especially preschoolers. And, asking them to "use their words" instead of fists assumes they have had opportunities to learn the appropriate words to use in various conflict situations.

In short, none of the solutions suggested above follow the principles and guidelines for Peaceable Classrooms used throughout this guide. A different approach is needed, one where adults help children learn how to think about their conflicts and what words to use to resolve their conflicts peacefully.

A Discussion on Working through Conflicts with Children

Here is how the teacher who intervened in Nathan and Delise's conflict helped them find a solution to their problem:

CONVERSATION

TEACHER: [Getting on his knees and putting a firm arm around each child's shoulders]

T: Delise and Nathan, you're both really upset.

T: What's the problem here?

NATHAN: Delise hit me!

DELISE: He gave me a needle—he hurt me.

NATHAN: I had to. I was the doctor!

T: Oh. You do have a problem. The doctor needs to give the patient a needle, but the patient doesn't want it—needles can hurt—and they can be scary, too.

DELISE: [Crying] I hate needles. They give you a lot of them in the hospital.

NATHAN: I had to—to stop your bleeding heart.

T: It sounds like you wanted to help Delise get better, Nathan, but needles upset Delise a lot. They feel very unsafe to her.

COMMENTARY

The teacher uses his body to try to calm the children and reassure them of their safety.

T. acknowledges their feelings without passing judgment.

He brings the focus onto defining the problem.

Nathan and Delise focus on the concrete aspects of the problem (the actual physical actions) from their own egocentric points of view, not as part of a shared problem.

T. helps the children define the problem as a shared one—in concrete terms from their two points of view.

This shows how Delise is bringing her experience into her play; knowing that can help others understand her point of view.

Nathan tries to explain his point of view. [He shows possible confusion between the real and unreal.]

T. acknowledges both children's legitimate desires. When a child believes his/her feelings/desires are acknowledged, the child is more willing to listen and try to understand the feelings/desires of the other person.

He also helps make logical causal connections between them. In this sense, T. acts as a "transformer"—someone who helps "static-thinkers" get from a cause to an effect.

T: Can you think of what you could do so you'll both feel safe and be happy. We need to figure something out so no one gets hurt.

T. focuses on coming up with a positive solution that feels okay to both children.

DELISE: I could be the doctor—not him.

Delise shows a typical pre-schooler's egocentric focus on one thing at a time—that is, what she wants.

T: So you could switch jobs—you be the doctor and Nathan the patient.

T. serves as a transformer for the children—helping them see how Delise's solution would affect both their actions.

NATHAN: I think I should use bandages.

Nathan focuses on what he (not Delise) can do, but his response does adapt to Delise's needs.

T: Tell me more. How would that work?

T. tries to get him to elaborate his ideas and think about how they could translate into practice.

NATHAN: Use bandages on her heart—no needles. I'll make her better that way. Catch the blood.

Nathan shows he has taken a lot of relevant information into account in his plan.

T: Uh-huh. You could find another way to make Delise's heart better—without a needle—so she wouldn't be scared of being hurt.

T. tries to make sure both children see how Nathan's solution would work and how it takes Delise's worries into account.

T: What do you think of that idea, Delise? Would that feel safe and okay to do?

T. tries to ensure both children can agree on this solution and will feel safe trying it.

DELISE: Good. I had lots of bandages when I was in the hospital. And Nathan puts them on good.

She can connect the solution to her experience—both in the hospital and with Nathan. This helps her assess the plan in advance of trying it.

T: Okay, it sounds like Delise wants to try that solution, too, Nathan. So let's try it. Make sure you let me know how it works.

T. asks the children to talk to him later which will provide them with an opportunity to evaluate how their plan worked.

T: Now, let's make sure you have the bandages you'll need before I leave. Which one do you need to use first, Nathan?

T. helps them begin to put their plan into action—preparing materials and figuring out what to do first.

[Later in the day at a class meeting, the teacher has Delise and Nathan talk about their problem and how they worked it out. He hoped to use this as a chance to extend all the children's thinking

Conversations don't always go in the direction a teacher plans. Based on the intensity of the children's interest in needles, T. decides to take the discussion in that direction.

about conflict, but instead the children all wanted to talk about their experiences with "needles."]

In keeping with the principles of a Peaceable Classroom, he respects the direction provided by the children, uses it to help them get new ideas for extending and elaborating their hospital play, and makes a note to himself to hold another conflict resolution discussion soon.

This teacher does much more than stop the children's conflict by treating it as a discipline or classroom management problem. Instead, by using the basic principles and practices that underlie a Peaceable Classroom, he helps Delise and Nathan actively build skills for resolving their conflicts peacefully.

- He *promotes a sense of safety and trust* by acknowledging both of their points of view as legitimate, by not casting blame, and by staying with the children until they find a solution that feels safe to both.

- He *helps the children feel responsible and capable* by encouraging them to express their ideas, involving them in the decision making, and showing them how their own egocentric ideas can work in their present situation.

- He *promotes mutual respect and interdependence* by helping them understand each other's point of view and how their actions and needs affect the other.

- He *helps both children develop skills for living and participating in a democratic community* by taking them through a process that teaches them the precursors of how to negotiate solutions to disagreements.

- Throughout, he *takes their developmental level and needs into account*. For instance, he helps the children understand each other's points of view and he fills in information and connections between ideas when their static thinking and lack of understanding of logical causality could stand in the way of a positive solution.

Teaching Children a "Win-Win" Approach to Conflict Resolution

This teacher is taking Delise and Nathan through a process of conflict resolution similar to that developed around the country for older children. In this process, the children seek a solution acceptable to everyone—a win-win solution. But as you can see, he has adapted this approach to the developmental level and needs of young children.

Here is the process the teacher used in helping Delise and Nathan resolve their conflict: 1) defining their problem, 2) finding a solution to which they can both agree, 3) helping them put their agreed-upon solution into practice, and 4) reflecting with them on how they feel it worked. (For a summary of this process, see Chart 5.1.)

Defining the problem

The first step in working through a conflict is defining the problem or conflict as a shared one, where there are two competing points of view. Because young children tend to focus on the most salient dramatic aspects of conflicts and their own egocentric wants and needs, they need help learning to see group problems and conflicts as dilemmas shared between two or more people. Until the children can do this, they will not look for a shared solution.

The way Delise and Nathan talk about their problem illustrates how most young children tend to think. They have a hard time seeing that their competing desires caused the problem—that Nathan's way of helping Delise scared her. So, when the teacher comes over, they define the problem in terms of static, concrete actions ("She hit me." "He gave me a needle. He hurt me."), not the underlying, less visible reasons for those actions.

Without assessing blame, the teacher helps the children see their problem as a shared one. He uses the concrete and visible aspects of the children's behavior to do so. Working within the confines of their egocentrism, he shows them they both have legitimate but incompatible points of view.

Brainstorming possible solutions and choosing one to try

The crucial part of the process is devising a range of possible solutions to the problem, figuring out how each possible solution might work, and then, choosing one to try. A solution should take into account both children's point of view, be agreeable to both, and restore a sense of safety. Such solutions are often called win-win solutions as opposed to win-lose solutions (where one child's position prevails) or lose-lose solutions (where both children end up losers). Many children have more experience with the last two types of solutions, and find them easier to use, especially because of the many solutions like these they see in the media.

Furthermore, coming up with win-win solutions is not easy for young children because of how they think. It requires such skills as taking both points of view into account, figuring out the logical causal connections between the problem and the solution, and thinking dynamically [imagining how to perform the transformation from one state of affairs (the problem) to another (the solution)]. But once they are helped to participate in the solution finding process, most children quickly learn to enjoy it and participate enthusiastically.

With the teacher's help, we see this process in action, when Delise and Nathan succeed at coming up with workable win-win solutions that are their own—either to change roles in the play or to change what the doctor does (use bandages instead of needles). The teacher helps them think through how their solution ideas would work but does not impose his own ideas about which is better. He makes sure both children agree that the solution they choose meets his criteria for win-win solutions—that both children want to try it and both feel safe with it.

Putting the "win-win" solution into practice

When children decide on a solution, they need a chance to see how it works. First, they need to come up with a plan for putting it into action, which is not an easy task for most young children. It involves figuring out what each needs to do to transform the situation from a problem or conflict into their agreed-upon solution. I have often seen young children devise good solutions like "We could take turns using that toy." But then they have a hard time figuring out what each of them has to do to actually take turns because they both assume they can go first.

As Delise and Nathan suggest solutions, the teacher helps them clarify what each plan might mean in action. Then, when they agree on one solution, they already have a good start for figuring out how to implement it. And when the teacher ends by focusing them on the bandages, he is actually guiding them through the transition from negotiation back to their play.

Reflecting on how the solution worked

Finally, children need a chance to evaluate their solutions after the solutions have been tried out—a time to reflect on how well their plan worked, how they feel about it, whether they would like to change anything about it, or try something new to improve it. Through evaluating their solutions children learn that problem solving is an ongoing process in which mistakes are okay and where they get better at finding effective solutions to their problems. Sharing what they learned with others not only helps children consolidate and expand on what they have learned and feel good about their accomplishments, it also provides a chance for children to reflect on how they each have contributed to creating a safe and caring classroom community.

Nathan and Delise's teacher provides just such an opportunity for all these things by making their conflict a discussion topic at a class meeting later in the day. This gives both children a chance to present their experience and tell how their solution worked. Unfortunately the discussion and input from others that could have helped them expand on their solution gets cut off by the group's interest in "needles." The teacher's decision to go with the children's apparent need to discuss needles illustrates the kind of flexibility and power-sharing that are constantly required in balancing the needs, interests, and goals of all the participants in a Peaceable Classroom.

When Your Efforts Do Not Seem to Work

Often, the children with "behavior problems"—those who most need help with the conflict resolution and other skills taught in Peaceable Classrooms—are also the ones who have the hardest time learning and using those skills. These are often likely to be the children who have been most affected by violence. They will frequenty demand the most help, take the most time, and need your best and most skillful thought and effort if they are to learn to participate in your Peaceable Classroom. They have a harder time and take longer to feel a sense of trust and safety in your classroom and have fewer skills for interacting positively with materials or other children. It can be difficult to stay with these children. They are the children who are often the hardest to have in your classroom. To the extent you can persevere, however, most of them will greatly benefit from your efforts.[3]

Even our most persistent and skillful efforts to help children learn to resolve their conflicts nonviolently cannot address all the problems that result from the violence and other stressors in their lives. All too often, these children are removed from group settings because they seem to need more intensive and far-reaching assistance than one or two teachers, working with a large group of children, can provide.[4] It is important to get these children the outside help they need to work through the trauma they may have experienced and develop the skills they need to function in a supportive group setting.

---

[3]For more information on working with children who may need more extensive assistance, see: *Challenging Behavior in Young Children: Understanding, Preventing, and Responding Effectively* by B. Kaiser and J. S. Rasminsky (Needham Heights, MA: Allyn and Bacon, 2003) and *A Matter of Trust: Connecting Teachers and Learners in the Early Childhood Clasasroom* by C. Howes and S. Ritchie (New York: Teachers College, 2002).

[4]For information on when to seek various types of outside help see *Children Who See Too Much* by B. M. Groves (Boston: Beacon Press, 2002).

Chart 5.1
SUMMARY OF PROBLEM SOLVING AND CONFLICT RESOLUTION PROCESS

Help Children:

• *Define the Problem as a Shared One.*
Because young children tend to focus on the most salient dramatic aspects of conflicts and their own egocentric wants and needs, they need help learning to see group problems and conflicts as dilemmas shared between two or more people.

• *Brainstorm Possible Solutions to the Problem.*
Coming up with a range of ideas for solving a problem that do not involve fighting poses a challenge which young children usually quickly learn to enjoy.

• *Figure Out How Each Possible Solution Might Work in Practice.*
Because they tend to focus on one thing at a time and have a hard time imagining what they cannot see, young children can have a hard time imagining how a solution will work in advance of actually trying it out. Helping children talk through the concrete actions involved with a solution puts them in a much better position to make an informed choice.

• *Choose a Solution Everyone Can Agree to Try.*
The goal here is to find a win-win solution where all children feel their point of view has been heard and respected.

• *Put their Solution into Practice.*
Children will often need help figuring out how to get started and coordinating their own actions with those of the others involved.

• *Evaluate How their Solution Worked and How to Make it Work Better.*
This helps children learn that problem solving is part of an ongoing process where mistakes are okay and where they can get better and better at finding effective solutions to their problems. It also provides an opportunity for children to reflect on how they each have contributed to creating a safe and caring classroom community.

At the same time, while there are limits to what you can do for these children, to the extent that they can feel safe and learn the skills and concepts needed to function in a Peaceable Classroom, they, too, will greatly benefit.

Guidelines for Practice

- When possible, spend the time needed to help children work through their conflicts using a win-win approach. Try to resist thinking of this work as interfering with teaching and learning.

- Plan your tasks and functions in the classroom so that at various times during each day you are performing a "floater" role—going from one independently functioning group of children to another to facilitate their interactions and activities. At these times you can work in depth with children who are having conflicts.

- Make sure children know they can rely on you to help them work through their conflicts nonviolently.

- Try to respect and incorporate the positive aspects of what children are learning about conflict resolution in their families into your efforts at conflict resolution in the classroom.

- Use children's efforts to work out their conflicts (both positively and negatively) as an opportunity to learn more about their current conflict resolution skills and needs.

- Find supportive adults in your school with whom to share and reflect on your conflict resolution efforts. For instance, you might form groups where members take turns bringing in examples of conflict resolution work for discussion, or observing and discussing how conflicts are dealt with in each other's classrooms.

- Keep in mind that the children who most need your help working through their conflicts are the ones most likely to benefit from it in the long run.

- Remember that some children will need more help than others learning to resolve their conflicts, especially in the beginning.

- Become familiar with the resources available in your school and community to which you can turn to get help for yourself and for the children whose needs around conflict cannot be fully met in a Peaceable Classroom.

Both Children and Teachers Are the Winners

One thing I've noticed above all else about children using the win-win approach to solving conflicts: most children seem to love doing it. They do not always say what an adult would like or expects them to say. And it is extremely difficult to figure out on the spot what to do and say next to move the problem-solving process along. Nevertheless, watching children learn this process has always left me feeling it is well worth the effort. Most children soon become fully engaged in the process of working out their conflicts, fully committed to trying out their solutions, and totally enthusiastic about sharing what they learned with their classmates.

Often, the children who most need help resolving their conflicts nonviolently respond to the win-

win approach the best. Perhaps, what we are teaching is more novel for these "discipline problems" than for children who have fewer problems with conflict—and therefore more interesting to them. Or perhaps they realize that the conflict resolution tools they are learning will help them feel better about themselves and empower them to interact with others in more positive, rather than the usual negative, ways. In either case, it gives these children the developmentally appropriate help they need to change their behavior.

Teaching conflict resolution to young children can also be rewarding for adults. In the long run, by using the time you currently spend on "disciplining" to help children learn the tools they need to resolve their conflicts peacefully, you will free up your own time to do other work in the classroom. You are more likely to feel the satisfaction that comes from seeing the positive effects of your own actions on children's development and behavior. Moreover, you will know you are teaching all children, whatever their degree of need, how to live as responsible and respectful members of a peaceable community.

Anti-Bias Education: Helping Children Understand and Appreciate Diversity

Four kindergartners are at the water table, giving the class baby dolls a bath. The dolls are racially diverse. The teacher notices that all four children are washing the white dolls. Kim announces she is "done" with her doll and begins to wash an African-American doll. Jinan says, "Yuk! She's dirty."

Children begin constructing ideas about similarities and differences among people very early in life.[1] The ideas they build are determined by what they see and hear about diversity in their immediate environment and in the wider society. Today, many of children's ideas about gender, race, special needs, and economic and ethnic diversity come from experience with news and entertainment media, toys, and popular culture, all of which are highly stereotyped.

Yet for children to become truly responsible and caring members of a global community where diverse people cooperate and resolve conflicts peacefully, a foundation needs to be laid early. The ideas about similarities and differences that children construct in the early years are the foundation upon which all later ideas on the subject must be built. Moreover, it is through helping young children develop critical thinking skills about justice and diversity, learning to respect and stand up for themselves and others in the face of injustice, and coming to a just and comfortable relationship with diversity among people, that they will develop the strategies they need to break the cycle of violence in their own lives and in the wider society.

It is important to recognize that the ideas children build from their experience will not be like those of adults. What they learn will depend on their current level of thinking as well as what they already have figured out from prior experience. As you can see from the examples of children expressing their ideas about similarities and differences in this chapter, when children feel safe to express their ideas openly, it is normal for them to not always say what we hope for or expect.

---

[1] For an expanded discussion of the issues raised in this chapter, see *The Anti-bias Curriculum: Tools for Empowering Young Children* by L. Derman-Sparks et al. (Washington, DC: National Association for the Education of Young Children, 1984) and *Teaching/Learning Anti-Racism: A Developmental Approach* by C. Phillips and L. Derman-Sparks (New York: Teachers College Press, 1997).

We have all heard a child make what seems like a negative or stereotyped comment about other people. Despite the values and attitudes we promote in our classrooms, I'm sure many of you have been seriously tempted in such situations to move away quietly, pretending you did not hear. It is often very difficult in such situations to know how to react and what to say. But in this case, doing nothing is doing something.

In the previous narrative, the teacher might have concluded that Jinan, the child who made the comment about the black doll, was racist—perhaps even that this is what she was taught at home (the "blaming the parent" approach). In such a case, she might have told the children to play with all the dolls because they all needed baths that day (the "color blind" approach)— thereby promoting the idea that all the dolls are equal and should be treated equally. She might have told them that the black doll was not dirty and given them factual information about skin color (the "teach children facts" approach). These responses attempt to deal directly with Jinan's apparently racist comment by pouring adult information about race and racism into the children's minds without helping them construct nonracist ideas through give-and-take dialogue.

A Teacher Helps Children Talk about Skin Color

What the teacher actually did reflects the principles and goals of Peaceable Classrooms. She went over to the water table and started washing an African-American doll herself and said to no one in particular, "I wonder what will happen if I scrub her really hard." The girls began to watch with apparent curiosity, commented that nothing changed, and then decided to try washing the dolls of color themselves to see if they could make anything happen if they "scrubbed really hard." When the teacher checked back a few minutes later, the girls reported in unison that they, too, could not get the dolls to change. In this way, she played the vital role of helping the children collect and use information about the dolls' skin color that challenged their idea that brown skin is dirty.

Because this was not the first time issues of race had come up in this teacher's classroom, she decided it was also important for the whole class to talk about "skin color" together. So she looked for an appropriate way to work the topic into a regular class meeting. She knew that in such a discussion it would be very important to keep the "safety rule" in mind for all the children when deciding how to respond to children's stereotyped comments. In other words, if what was said threatened the sense of safety of another child, it would be vital to deal with it directly and quickly, using the safety rule as a guide. The biggest challenge would be to respond in a way that respected and supported both childrens' sense of safety.

Here is the teacher's account of what happened:

That day at class meeting, the children were taking turns telling stories about their "family pictures" (family photographs each child had brought in from home). One child commented that her mother was white and her father was black, and that's why she was brown. All the children began to look at their skin and the skin of their friends.

A child sitting near a friend called out with great excitement, "We have the same color, so we're best friends."

I asked him if he thought they were best friends because they were the same color or because they shared similar interests. He said he thought it was because they were both white.

I wondered aloud if you could like someone who had a different skin color. Immediately, one of the children said with great authority, "Of course. Otherwise, my mom couldn't like me because she's white and I'm tan."

Another child jumped in: "I think you like to play with the one that's your color. I play with the white baby (in the dramatic play area)."

When I asked them for further explanation, someone said, "You like your color best, so that's who you play with."

A white girl explained that "if you're having a baby, you usually have one the color that you're like."

Soon after, a biracial child jumped in to say everyone should play with all the colors of baby dolls, pointing out that sometimes baby brothers and sisters look different from each other and parents still love them.

The children expressed their ideas and concerns for a long time. "What if a lady with white skin wanted to throw her baby away because it had a different color skin? I wouldn't throw my baby away."

"You can't have a black baby if you're white, but there's something called mixed, and it could be mixed."

"Well I change in the summer so then I'm mixed too."

"I think you are what you are, and that's it."

I have been teaching for a long time and think I'm really good at talking with kids about hard and complicated issues. But this was one of the hardest discussions I've ever had. I never knew what I would have to deal with next. I always had to make sure on the spot, after each comment, that everyone felt safe. I worked hard to make sure all the children felt safe saying what they thought but I worried that comments might be made that hurt other children. You know, the most important thing to me about my teaching is that the classroom is a safe and trusting place for children. I would probably never have a discussion like this early in the school year (it occurred in April).

But at this point in the year, a sense of community is really building among us all. An important part of that community is the children feeling safe asking questions, making observations, and talking about hard issues. The kids said things that are, or at least seem, racist. But it was important to me to get their ideas out in a way that let us explore and change them.

This teacher is describing how she used a give-and-take dialogue to help children express their thinking and build new ideas about skin color. She facilitated the discussion by:

- maintaining a climate of safety and respect, where children feel comfortable asking questions and honestly expressing their ideas and concerns;

- listening to and accepting what the children say, even when what they say seems, from an adult's point of view, to reflect stereotypes;

- helping the children use their prior experiences to discuss and clarify their thinking about this issue;

- trying not to characterize answers as right or wrong or merely tell children the right way to think about skin color;

- challenging and complicating the children's thinking about skin color without directly bringing in her own adult thinking on the subject; and

- using the discussion as part of an ongoing process of gradually constructing an understanding and appreciation of skin color and race.

A Letter to Parents about a Special Needs Curriculum

Here is a letter the same teacher sent to the parents of the children in her classroom after the dialogue took place. In order to build bridges between the home and school, she often wrote to parents about what was happening in school. This letter describes the special needs curriculum. It illustrates teaching about diversity using the same underlying principles and practices she used in the above example. In addition, the teacher shows parents how their children are learning about differences among people, as well as how she is teaching more traditional skills (like reading, writing, science) as she builds curriculum activities around the children's needs, interests, and various levels of understanding.

Dear Kindergarten Parents,

The classroom continues to be a busy place. It's really exciting to watch the group at this point in the year. The children are so comfortable with each other, with the routines, with the expectations, and with themselves. It seemed like a good time to expand our horizons.

So a few weeks back, we began to look at people with physical differences. The kids seemed enthralled by the biography of Louis Braille and became very interested in Braille writing. We began to experiment, using a stylus to "write" in Braille. Then, we read *Mine for a Year*, a book about a child who takes care of a puppy that is going to be trained as a guide dog.

This experience came alive when Hernandez and his dad invited a blind neighbor to visit our classroom. Pete and his guide dog, Victor, spent an afternoon choice time with us. The kids had prepared questions for Pete ahead of time, and he had prepared a little presentation for the kids, too.

I wish you could have seen the interactions between the kids and Pete. Their questions reflected a variety of issues. Some had come up from our reading. Others seemed to reflect the kids' feelings and curiosities ("What does it feel like to be blind?" "Have you been blind all your life?" "How did you get blind?" "Can't the doctor fix your eyes?" "How do you think about colors?"). Pete was truly wonderful. He answered their questions openly and honestly. I think each child was impressed by how similar Pete's life was to their own. He totally wowed them with all of his special "gadgets," such as his talking watch and talking calculator.

After our discussion, he stayed for the remainder of choice time. I'm left with the memory of Pete reading *Stone Soup* (Braille adapted) aloud, with Victor and a few children stretched out at his feet and the classroom slowly growing quiet as more and more kids drifted into the meeting area to listen to this familiar story read by a new friend in a new way.

Pete and Victor's visit was a special time for all of us. This week, we have sent them two class thank-you "notes," one that we recorded on an audio tape and one that is a Braille version of the same message—a new kind of writing lesson!

One extension of our work on blindness and deafness in the upcoming weeks will be to talk about how your eyes and ears work. We are planning a visit by a physician to help us understand these parts of our body. You'll hear more about that later.

Sincerely,

T.

What Anti-Bias Education Is

These examples of building curricula around skin color and special needs show anti-bias education in action in a Peaceable Classroom. Anti-bias education:

- helps children gradually construct a stereotype- and bias-free understanding of people's similarities and differences;

- incorporates all aspects of diversity—from gender, race, economic class, and ethnic background to physical, intellectual, and emotional characteristics to thoughts and feelings and personal likes and dislikes—and includes what is sometimes termed multicultural education, but goes beyond it;

- informs all the interactions in Peaceable Classrooms because what children learn about how to treat others is highly influenced by how they deal with diversity among people and how they understand themselves as fitting into a global context;

- is essential if children are to feel truly safe and fully valued in a classroom, for if the whole range of appearances, experiences, thoughts, and feelings of one child are not respected, then any child can also feel vulnerable because of who she or he is;

- teaches children, at a developmentally appropriate level, how to take concrete social action that promotes greater social equality and justice; and

- constitutes what should be happening in the early childhood curriculum for the subject traditionally called social studies—but is infused into daily classroom life, not taught at an isolated time or as a prescribed set of facts.

What Anti-Bias Education Is Not

Thinking about what anti-bias education is not can help to further clarify what it is. It is not:

- pretending to be "color-blind" or treating all children as if they were exactly alike and ignoring who they are as individuals, in all their uniqueness and diversity;

- preaching adult ideas to children about how to think about similarities and differences among people, because children need to build ideas actively from their own experience;

- teaching children only about cultures other than their own (as multicultural education is often practiced).

Anti-Bias Education Poses Special Challenges for Teachers

While anti-bias education is at the heart of effective teaching about peace and conflict, it still presents one of the most difficult challenges Peaceable Classroom teachers face. There are a number of reasons anti-bias education is challenging:

- Because many of us rarely talk about these issues ourselves, we have few experiences to guide us in our work with children.

- Anti-bias education carries the constant risk of children raising uncomfortable issues (e.g., liking people best who are the same skin color as oneself).

- The discussion can go in unpredictable directions (e.g., children bringing up skin color in a discussion of family photos, when there are so many other things to discuss about the photos).

- Moreover, because young children think so differently from adults about diversity, when they feel safe enough to say what they really think (not what they think adults want to hear), it is not always what we are comfortable hearing. They will often talk about similarities and differences in what seem like stereotypes to adults. However, sometimes the most outrageous statement can really be a question—an effort to get guidance, information, and a thoughtful response or answer from trusted adults.

How Young Children Think about Similarities and Differences

As with all aspects of the curriculum in Peaceable Classrooms, the way young children think plays a crucial role in how we can best help them develop an understanding and respect for diversity. The same characteristics of thinking that affect how young children understand other concepts of peace, violence, and conflict (as discussed in Chapter 2) also affect how their ideas about similarities and differences develop.

- **Children begin to construct ideas about similarities and differences when they are very young.** Almost from birth, children learn by noticing differences. They use similarities and differences among people, objects, and events to help them define and understand their world—learning, for example, to differentiate a parent from a stranger, a bottle from a breast, or a rattle from a pacifier. They learn a label for their gender at around two years old, after which they start building an understanding of what it means to be a boy or girl—like me or not like me. By three they have begun to develop ideas about race and special needs.

- **Young children tend to focus on one thing at a time—usually, in this case, the most salient and visible aspects of similarities and differences among people.** This means that children will most likely focus on skin color to determine race and hair length or clothing (rather than genitals) to determine gender. With special needs, visible and concrete aspects of a disability—a blind person using a guide dog, for instance—will be more relevant and interesting to the child than less visible ones, such as the physiological reasons why the person cannot see.

- **Young children tend to think in dichotomies.** Someone is either one thing or the other (but not both) and thus either "like me" or "not like me." Subtle variations and shades of gray are harder for them to understand. This can lead to thinking in stereotypes. In the incident described above, the children struggle with differences in skin color that do not fit into simple dichotomous categories—a child who has neither his mother's nor his father's skin color.

- **Young children generally think egocentrically and concretely—relating what they see and hear about similarities and differences to themselves and their own experience.** The children discussing skin color above constantly refer to their experience with skin color as a basis for drawing conclusions about race.

- **Static thinking can make it hard for young children to understand logical causal relationships or the permanence of physical characteristics.** It will be several more years before they realize these characteristics are unchangeable. This can lead to misunderstandings about similarities and differences—for instance, that washing will change skin color or growing longer hair can change a boy into a girl. It can also lead children to make illogical causal connections—for instance, that skin color determines friendships.

- **Children's ideas about diversity and how they learn to respond to it are influenced by what they see and hear in the world around them about similarities and differences.** Because society—for instance through entertainment media—provides them with an abundance of stereotyped content to use in constructing their ideas about such differences as race and gender, it can be difficult to sort out which of children's ideas result from how they think and which result from what they have seen and heard.

Guidelines for Practice

- Focus both on similarities (what brings people together and what they share) and differences. For instance, eating meals with a variety of different implements (i.e., forks, spoons, chopsticks, fingers) can help children learn that all people eat but in many different ways.

- Start with a focus on the concrete aspects of similarities and differences—what children can see. The "Class Graphs" in Chapter 9 show some ways to do this.

- Focus on similarities and differences that are connected to the children's experiences. For instance, young children discussing gender issues will be more interested in talking about the toys girls and boys use than reproduction.

- Try to utilize whatever examples of diversity the children and adults in your setting provide. Even groups that at first glance appear quite homogeneous can offer children many opportunities to experience a wide range of diversity. Food preferences, hair color and length, family size, and favorite stuffed animals all provide a meaningful basis for teaching young children about similarities and differences.

- If your classroom lacks racial, ethnic, or economic diversity, make sure to find meaningful ways to help expand children's experience in these areas. Books, photographs, music, art, cooking, dolls, posters, class visitors, and field trips are just a few ways you can begin.

- Provide children many opportunities to experience directly the value diversity can have in their daily lives. This can help transform their tendency to treat differences with suspicion and intolerance. The "Class Graphs" described in Chapter 9 provide a highly engaging and developmentally appropriate way to begin.

- Children learn by noticing differences. Rather than treating their focus on diversity as something to be avoided, try to use it as a tool to help engage them in a wide range of activities. The narratives at the beginning of this chapter provide highly successful examples of this approach.

- Challenge children's stereotypes, including those stereotypes they learn from the wider society and the media. This is often best done by introducing information that contradicts and complicates thinking in stereotypes, as the classroom examples in this chapter illustrate.

- Remember to keep the "safety rule" in mind when deciding how to respond to children's stereotyped comments. If what is said threatens the sense of safety of another child, it is vital that you deal with this directly and quickly using the safety rule to guide you. It is also important to deal with it in a way that respects the child who made the comment. Because of how young children think, they often may not realize the hurtful impact their stereotyped comments might have on another child.

- Rather than feeling you always have to "fix" children's stereotyped ideas or immediately answer all their questions about diversity, focus on helping them express their diverse ideas and provide feedback to each other. This can encourage them to share the responsibility of creating an anti-biased classroom, and through their participation, actively break down stereotyped and biased ideas.

A Group Discussion to Expand Gender Roles

The two examples at the beginning of this chapter show how anti-bias education can be built into the curriculum of Peaceable Classrooms. Here is an example of the kind of give-and-take, problem-solving dialogue you can use around any diversity issue. In this case, a teacher of four-year-olds is working on gender bias with the children in her classroom.

CONVERSATION	COMMENTARY
TEACHER: I've been noticing something in the classroom that hasn't felt so good to me. I've noticed that only boys have been playing in the block area.	The teacher presents the topic to the class as a problem to be solved. In this sense, she uses the meeting to take the children through a problem-solving sequence similar to the one for resolving conflicts described in the preceding chapter.
T: You know how we've talked before about how it's important to do all the activities around the classroom.	She tries to help the children connect to prior experience and knowledge.
T: I wonder if you have any ideas about this—why don't the girls choose blocks?	She immediately gets the children to express their ideas, even if there is a risk of hearing responses that express stereotypes.
HENRY: Boys like using blocks more.	Possible egocentrism. And he focuses on only one aspect of the situation. Also, he seems to be dividing boys and girls up into two dichotomous categories.
HELEN: Boys always sign up first. There's never any room in blocks.	She is making a logical causal connection.
T: So sometimes when girls want to sign up, the boys have already taken all the spaces on the choice board? I know blocks are really popular with a lot of boys.	Without judging them, T. elaborates on one child's ideas. In this way she serves as the intermediary between the speaker and the other children.
JOSH: Yeah, boys are better.	He is stating an opinion that may or may not be a stereotype.
T: You think the boys are better. Can you say more about that? How are boys better?	T. asks an open-ended question to determine if he's thinking in stereotypes.

JOSH: Boys are better in the blocks.

T: Oh, I see. You think boys are better with the blocks. Does any one else have anything to say about that?

T. tries to elicit comments that could contradict or complicate his thinking about a stereotype.

JOYCE: They are better. The boys use them more so they're better.

This may not be what T. expected to hear, but it does elaborate on the issue. And it indicates the child's perceptions and sense of causality.

T: So you think if you use blocks a lot, it helps you get better, and boys use them more than girls. Anyone else?

T. emphasizes Joyce's causal connection between experience and expertise; this might help the girls realize what they need to do to get better at blocks.

SHEILA: That's 'cause the boys never let us use the blocks.

Here is another causal connection. Many of these children clearly are comfortable saying what they think.

JENNY: Yeah, they use all the blocks. We never get enough to do what we want. [Several girls nod in agreement, while boys start to mumble objections.]

Clearly, a lot of tension has built up between the girls and boys over blocks. T. seems to have tapped into a valuable issue for the children to work on.

T: It sounds like some of the girls don't feel very good about going into the block area. Can anyone say more about that?

T. acknowledges and validates the feelings. While she makes sure the children know she is still in charge and keeping things safe, she is giving them a lot of room to explore and understand the problem.

KAMIKO: I never sign up for blocks—boys won't let you build what you want.

She focuses on one key aspect of the situation.

HENRY: They can't do it right. They wreck our buildings. Yesterday they wrecked my marble run. It fell.

Both boys and girls seem able to provide negative feedback to each other without hurting feelings of individual children.

T: Well, I can tell from what all of you have said that we do have a problem. You all seem to have complaints about what happens when boys and girls are together in blocks—the girls don't feel very comfortable or safe building when boys are there, and some boys don't feel like things work very well when girls are there. [Most children nod in agreement.]

T. summarizes the problem and tries to help. The children see it as a shared problem when is it presented from both the girls' and the boys' points of view.

T: Who has any ideas about what we can do so the boys and girls can both play in the blocks and feel good about it?

T. now shifts the discussion to finding a win-win solution that can work for all the children.

JAMAL: Both take turns.

Jamal offers a static idea without any sense of what it might mean in practice.

T: How would that work?

T. asks child to elaborate his idea for others.

JAMAL: You could have boys use blocks one day and girls use blocks one day.

The beginning of incorporating two different ideas in a dynamic—rather than static—way.

KAREN: Two boys and two girls.

She is modifying Jamal's idea.

T: That's another way to share. Jamal's idea is that we take turns by having one day when boys go in and the next day when girls go. Karen's idea has two girls and two boys—since four kids can go in blocks at a time, we could have half and half. Any other ideas?

T. again acts as an interpreter, helping the children see their different ideas about how to put a "turn-taking" solution into practice.

JULIE: Partners.

A potential solution, but it's expressed egocentrically, so other children might not understand what she means.

T: Can you say more?

JULIE: Yup. Girl and boy partner to build. They have to build together.

The teacher's previous efforts to model ways of working together with the children has helped them come up with possible solutions here.

HENRY: Boys could teach them things.

Henry clearly likes this solution and has ideas about how it might work. Here he is referring back to the earlier idea that boys are better at blocks and incorporating it into the solution.

T: You mean partners could help each other learn things—like Henry, you're good at marble runs and Josh, you love towers?

T. tries to stress the idea of helping others by sharing special skills. This gives the children concrete ideas about how they might successfully work together.

[Several children seem to be nodding in approval, but a few also seem to be getting restless. T. decides to speed up.]

This has been a long discussion for children this age. T. needs to decide how to pace things to take into account the needs and attention spans of all the children.

T: That last solution reminds me of when we've talked before about ways we can teach each other new things. Raise your hand if it feels okay to try having partners. [Most children raise their hands.]

T: Okay. We'll try partners. But let's make sure we check in with each other in a few days to see how it's working. We need to stop now, but tomorrow, before sign-up time, we'll talk about how to choose partners.

T. decides to go with this solution. She bases her choice on the apparent interest of many of the children in this solution, and she checks with the children to make sure they agree this is a win-win solution.

Before they end, T. makes sure the children know what comes next in this problem-solving process— how to translate the solution into practice.

A Special Problem of Gender Stereotyping and Sexual Content in the Media

The lessons children learn when they are young about what it means to be a male and female and about the nature of relationships between them will become part of the foundation they will use for developing relationships when they grow up.[2] In recent years, I have heard increasingly worrisome stories from teachers and parents about how the gender stereotyping and sexual content children see in the media is playing out in children's attitudes and behavior. For instance, parents report girls who only want pretend make-up and shirts exposing their midrifts as gifts for their fifth birthday and who cry when they are in the bathtub because they are not skinny like the very thin and popular girls in their class at school. Teachers describe girls acting out Brittany Spears' sexual gyrations and mouthing the words of her songs and boys pretending to be professional wrestlers pretending to slug other boys and girls as they make sexual comments (that they probably don't fully understand) like "come get some" and "do you want a piece of me?" Both girls and boys in first and second grade have come home asking about sexual terminology they have heard such as French kissing, blow jobs, and rape.

Ever since the deregulation of children's television in 1984, gender stereotypes in the media and in media-linked toys have become increasingly rigid and extreme. For the most part, boys see over and over that they need to have big muscles, be strong, powerful, independent, and ready to use vioence to solve their problems. Girls are conditioned to be nice, dependent, and especially focused on appearance—i.e., being pretty, unhealthily thin, and wearing the "right" clothes.

Along with these stereotypes are increasingly sexualized images of males and females, images of sexy behavior, and even sex are increasingly prevalent in media culture. In fact, a recent study by the Kaiser Family Foundation found that two out of three shows on TV include sexual content, an increase from about half of all shows in the 1997-1998 television season. In addition, much of the sexual behavior on the screen is also connected to violence—including muscle-bound men attacking sexily-dressed women. These images can dehumanize relationships between females and males, and instead of modeling positive and caring relationships, encourage the victimization of women by men.

The following examples of children's toy boxes, which are marketed to children as young as three years old, represent only a small fraction of the kinds of stereotypes children are confronted with today. Young children are especially vulnerable to confusion and negative influences from such depictions of stereotyped gender roles and sex. They are looking for clearly identifiable information to figure out

[2] For more information on this issue see: *Human Sexuality Development: A Guide for Early Childhood Educators and Families* by K. Chrisman and D. Couchenour. (Washington, DC: National Association for the Education of Young Children, 2002.)

These action figure toys illustrate how gender and ethnic stereotypes are linked to many toys of violence that permeate children's popular culture.

[right] Figure 6.1: This World Wrestling Federation (now World Wrestling Entertainment) figure of the real female character Sable is recommended for children ages 4 and up. Sable comes equipped with a whip, a chair, spiked high-heeled shoes, and simulated leather pants and bra (unzipped in the front).

[below right] Figure 6.2: The back of the Sable toy box advertises male action figures such as Al Snow, who is holding the severed head of a woman, and B.A. Billy Gunn, who has red lipstick marks on his boxer shorts (the biggest being over his genitals). The linking of sex and violence is an increasingly common phenomenon in childhood popular culture.

[below left] Figure 6.3: These Fisher-Price Great Adventure Bandits, recommended for children ages 3 and up, have stereotypical Arab features and carry multiple weapons.

what it means to be a boy or a girl. Just as with violence, because of how they think, they are drawn to the salient and dramatic cues they see on the screen. They will tend to focus on how the sexual behavior looks without understanding much about the underlying feeling and affection that accompanies male and female (including sexual) relationships. Therefore, it seems reasonable to predict that what children are learning about gender roles and sex from the media culture will have a negative impact on the the kinds of relationships they will establish as adults and how they will view violence, peace, and conflict within these relationships.

Just as children need the help of adults in sorting out the violence that enters their lives, they also need our help dealing with what they see and hear about gender stereotypes and sexual behavior. In thinking about how to do this, you will find that the basic guidelines suggested for dealing with violence in Peaceable Classrooms will provide the starting points you will need to make sense of these issues too—especially helping children know that it is safe to raise these issues with you and that you will help them sort out what they hear. In the words of one mother with whom I recently spoke, "Maybe I was naive, but I didn't expect to be talking about rape with my seven-year-old daughter until she was in her teens. But, as uncomfortable as I felt when she asked me about it, I was really glad that she knew that if she had questions, I was the one she could safely ask."

Anti-Bias Education: The Heart of Peace Education in the Early Years

Infusing anti-bias education into all aspects of the Peaceable Classroom poses an enormous challenge. Society is more diverse than ever before, as are children in early childhood settings. As discussed, young children are predisposed to interpret similarities and differences among people in stereotyped ways. Add to this the fact that from very early in life children are exposed to many examples of racism, sexism, classism, and other stereotypes, as well as vast amounts of violent imagery, both real and pretend, where people who are different hurt each other. This teaches children that differences among people are a justifiable cause for violence. Much work needs to be done to create a society which models respect for diversity for children. We still have a lot to learn about what developmentally appropriate anti-bias education might look like. At the same time, we know enough to make a meaningful start. Perhaps even more than with any other aspect of Peaceable Classrooms, effective anti-bias education requires that you continually forge new responses and approaches based on the immediate demands and needs of your particular group of children.

7

Fostering Creative Play in the Media Age: Strategies for Responding to War and Superhero Play

Margaret, an experienced preschool teacher, recently wrote, "I need recommendations on how to help preschool children who are caught up with superheroes and gun play and use play time to create problems in the classroom. Four-year-old Jules is particularly obsessed. Telling him no guns or pretend fighting just does not work; he argues that he's a Power Ranger and needs to fight the bad guys. When he's a good guy he seems to think it is okay to use whatever force is needed to suppress the bad guy 'because that's what a superhero does!' And then someone, usually a bad guy, ends up getting hurt. When we try to enforce a ban, the children make up a story about it being some situation other than superhero play.

"These children, especially Jules, don't seem to know ways to play that are more conducive to building friendships and learning how to get along with others. They also seem to play the same thing over and over without having any new ideas of their own."

The Impact of Entertainment Violence on Children's Play[1]

Media is playing an increasingly prominent role in children's lives. It is used as a vehicle for marketing a vast consumer culture to children, including media-linked toys. One of the most worrisome aspects of media culture is the large quantity of just-for-fun violence, mean-spirited behavior, and stereotypes to which children are exposed. A growing body of research supports the notion that media violence is harming children and contributing to violence in society.

The violent media culture is having an especially negative impact on the play of many young children. Children have less time to play than in the past, in part because of the time they spend in front of the television. Then, when they do play, what they play and how they play, as seen in the concerns voiced by the childcare consultant above, are often highly influenced by what they have seen on the screen. The lines of realistic toys (like the toys whose boxes are shown in Figures 7.1 and 7.2) marketed to accompany TV shows, movies, and video games encourage children to act out or imitate the

---

[1]This chapter focuses primarily on play connected to entertainment violence and media-linked war toys. For an expanded discussion see *Who's Calling the Shots? How to Respond Effectively with Children's Fascination with War Play and War Toys* by N. Carlsson-Paige and D.E. Levin (Gabriola Island, BC, CAN: New Society Publishers, 1990); *The War Play Dilemma: Balancing Needs and Values in the Early Childhood Classroom* by N. Carlsson-Paige and D.E. Levin (New York: Teachers College Press, 1987); and, *Under Dead Man's Skin: Discovering the Meaning of Children's Violent Play* by J. Katch (Boston: Beacon Press, 2001). For an expanded discussion of war play connected to violence in the news, see chapter eight of this book and "Beyond Banning War and Superhero Play: Meeting Children's Needs in Violent Times," by D.E. Levin, *Young Children* (May 2003).

violence, stereotyped behavior, and attitudes they see on the screen. The situation is compounded by the rise of increasingly violent video games—an industry that collects the bulk of toy-buying dollars these days. Although video games are often called toys, they promote little, if any, constructive play, and recent research is pointing to their potential role in contributing to violent behavior.[2]

The Importance of Play

Play is vital to all aspects of children's healthy development and learning. Children actively use play to master experience, to try out new skills and ideas, and to feel powerful and strong. In their play, children find interesting problems to work on, learn how to solve them in creative ways, and experience the sense of power that can come from actively working out an idea, problem, or skill on their own.

The subject matter children bring to their play can give us a window into understanding what they are interested in, what they may already know, as well as what they are struggling to understand. When children see a lot of violence—be it entertainment or real—it is natural for them to bring it into their play to try to make meaning. So it is not surprising that when children are exposed to a lot of media violence, adults report children's efforts to bring that violence into their play.

The content of children's play also influences the lessons they learn from their play. When a lot of the content is about caring and nurturing others, then children will learn lessons about positive social relationships. On the other hand, when much of the content is violent, then they will be learning lessons about violence.

What exactly children learn about violence as they play will depend on how they play. That is, the lessons learned from play with violence are influenced by how much children are able to transform violent content into creative play and by how much the play is narrowly scripted and stuck on mere imitation of the violence seen on the screen.

Changes in Play: From Play to Imitation

I have often heard concerns like those expressed by the childcare consultant above about media-influenced play that abruptly ends when someone gets hurt or breaks down into tears. I also hear that the children who seem most obsessed by war and superhero play are the same children who seem to have the hardest time engaging in creative and imaginative play of their own design. This apparent change in children's play can have serious ramifications for children's behavior, their learning process, and teachers' roles and responsibilities.

First, many teachers say they spend an increasing amount of time entering into play situations to discipline—rather than facilitate. They spend time setting limits and even redirecting children away from their play, helping hurt and crying children, and mediating disputes among children. With these kinds of problems accelerating, play—which has been viewed for decades as an essential part of the fabric of early childhood classrooms—has become a problem in many classrooms and even something to be avoided.

Second, many children are being deprived of needed opportunities to engage in rich and meaningful play, an essential component of healthy development and growth. In play, children use their creativity and imagination to transform experience into something uniquely meaningful for each person. As they do so, their sense of emotional control, mastery, and well-being is enhanced, as is their intellectual understanding.

[2]For instance, see: "The Effects of Violent Video Games on Aggressive Behavior, Aggressive Cognition, Aggressive Affect, Physiological Arousal, and Prosocial Behavior: A Meta-Analytic Review of the Scientific Literature" by C.A. Anderson and B.J. Bushman, *Psychological Science* 12:5 (September, 2001): 353-359; and, "How Violent Video Games May Violate Children's Health" by E. Hae-Jung Song and J.E. Anderson, *Contemporary Pediatrics* 18:5 (May, 2001): 102-120.

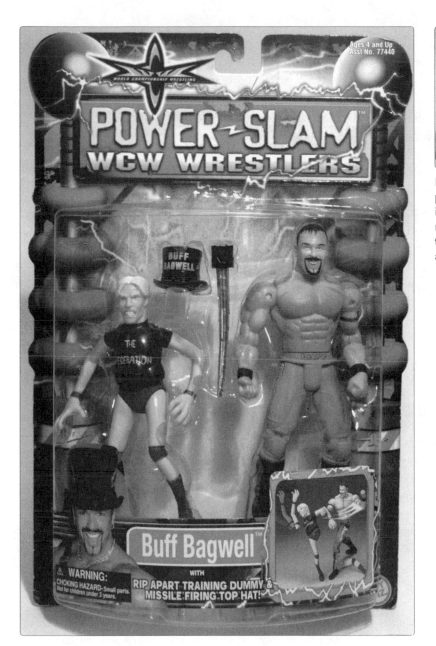

Figures 7.1 and 7.2: Here are examples of single-purpose toys that can channel children into imitating violence in their play. Both are linked to violent media (Jurassic Park and Professional Wrestling) that has content rated for older children than the age recommendations on the toy boxes.

For play to serve development, children need to be in charge of what happens—to be their own scriptwriter, director, producer, actor, costumer, set designer, and prop person. For instance, when children play "house," each child brings his or her own unique experiences, needs, concerns, and questions into the play—how and what to prepare for pretend meals, how to talk to each other as they pretend to eat, how to work on disagreements that arise, and how to feed the "baby" (doll). Thus, no two children's house play scenarios should ever look exactly the same, and each child's play should evolve and change over time in unique ways.

But media-influenced play can undermine this deeply personal process. For instance, when Jules and his friends are playing Power Rangers, rather than becoming involved in their play as a unique and exciting script, the children seem only able to focus on the idea that good guys fight with and beat bad guys— the center theme of the TV program they have learned to imitate and enjoy most. As a result, the play quickly deteriorates; children end up scared and hurt; none of the children receive the wide range of benefits that would have resulted from more sustained and elaborated play; and the safety rule is violated.

Today, many young children spend a lot of their play time engaged in this kind of media-influenced imitative play rather than creative play when they generate the scenarios themselves. Thus, the opportunities for their play to serve their development and learning can be seriously diminished. In this situation, as elaborated below, children run a serious risk of never learning to create deeply meaningful and growth-producing play and of learning the harmful lessons about violence they imitate in their play.

How Development and Learning Are Undermined[3]

- Intellectual development is threatened when children are deprived of the kind of play that helps them use content from their direct experience to construct new and more advanced ideas and skills. In addition, as the whole process of play is undermined, so are children's opportunities to develop creativity and imagination, problem-solving skills, the ability to take risks and try out new ideas, and the confidence that they can solve problems and master academic skills on their own.

- Media-scripted imitative play can seriously impair children's social development. When children are following someone else's script about how to treat others, they are not engaging in the kind of active, social knowledge building necessary to develop a broad repertoire of increasingly advanced social understandings and skills. Instead, when much of the behavior in the script children are imitating is violent, they cannot help but learn a repertoire of violent and antisocial behavior. Furthermore, because much of the media content children bring to their imitative play contains gender, racial, and ethnic stereotypes, they will use their play to internalize these messages. This can contribute to stereotyped behavior, mistrust, and intolerance toward differences among people.

- Children's emotional development can also be affected. Imitative play offers children few chances to experience the satisfaction and power that can come from working something out in a personally meaningful and creative way. Being deprived of the deep satisfaction of play can lead children to look outside themselves for satisfaction and make them susceptible to the influence of others (i.e., peers, TV characters, advertisers, etc.). In addition, since elaborate play provides children with endless opportunities to develop a sense of competence and confidence in their ability to affect the world, failure to engage in such play can contribute to a sense of disempowerment and impotence. Children who feel impotent are more likely to mimic the violence they see on the screen in order to feel powerful.

---

[3]For a more detailed discussion of this issue see: "Endangered Play, Endangered Development: A Constructivist View of the Role of Play in Development and Learning" by D.E. Levin in *Playing for Keeps*, ed. A. Phillips (St. Paul, MN: Red Leaf Press, 1996).

Developing an Approach to Deal with War and Superhero Play

Because so many early childhood teachers recognize that play with violence has little value for children (and some even worry it can harm them), and because violent episodes often cause havoc in classrooms, it is easy to make compelling arguments for banning the play. Yet many of those who try to enforce a "no war and weapons play (or pretend fighting) at school" rule face a constant struggle. Some say that they end up feeling uncomfortable as guerrilla wars erupt with children sneaking around the room or playground, trying to hide this kind of play from adults, and turning their snack crackers into pretend guns which are then gobbled up before they can be accused of violating the "no guns in school" rule.

It is not at all surprising that content from entertainment media is so central to children's play, and therefore, so hard for adults to ban. Children bring the most salient and graphic aspects of their experience to their play—the content they are struggling most to work out and understand and that promises to be the most exciting and powerful. Yet because children usually imitate the violent parts of media content over and over instead of creatively working out their own solutions and understandings, the issues they bring to this kind of play are rarely adequately resolved.

Working to ban media-controlled imitative play, or even just to contain it, can be an appropriate stopgap measure when the problems created by the play become too great or the safety rule is violated. However, for children to work through their deep issues and needs in a meaningful way, they will usually require much more direct help from adults.

The teacher in Chapter 3 ("Setting the Stage"), who talks with the children about how to deal with the problems that arise from the toy guns that are made from scrounge materials, provides one important alternative model for what we can do—other than simply banning the play—that respects children's interests and needs. If the children agreed on a solution to try such a model and then found that some children were still getting upset and not feeling safe, then the teacher would need to call another meeting to discuss the problem. She might impose a ban on the play, explaining that it was the only way to make sure all the children felt safe. Then, if the children tried to sneak around and violate the ban, the teacher would need to refer back to what the children had learned about why the play was banned and help them figure out what would help them follow the ban.

The principles of Peaceable Classrooms discussed throughout this book provide the foundation you will need for developing an approach for dealing with war, weapons, and superhero play which respects children's needs, gives them a voice, furthers their learning about being positive social beings, and keeps them safe. Whatever you do, it will be important to keep in mind that:

- Whether within or outside of play, children need help from adults in working through the issues raised by violent and disturbing content in the media. Merely banning the play does not give children the help they need and can even increase the harmful impact of the violence. This leaves it up to the children themselves to make their own meaning from the entertainment violence they see—without the benefit of input from a caring adult. It can also leave children feeling unsafe— seeing the world as a dangerous place—where fighting, weapons, and super powers are necessary to keep oneself safe.

- Many children also need adults to help them learn how to engage in rich and meaningful play, the kind of play that optimally serves their development. Not being a "good player" deprives children of one of the most powerful vehicles they have available for working through the issues raised by violence.

- Children who have experienced violence in their own lives will be the ones who most need play to work out their issues. They may also be the ones who have the hardest time engaging in this kind of play because so much of their energy has had to go into protecting themselves from frightening experiences. Therefore, while it will not be easy, it is especially critical that teachers support and facilitate the kind of play that can help these children meet the social, emotional, and intellectual challenges resulting from their experiences with violence.[4] We will need support, training, and resources to learn how to do this well.

- Parents need help learning how to work with their children to combat the hazards of media culture and to negotiate the minefields of violent media. The more you can work together with parents to help them actively choose appropriate media for their children, limit their children's exposure to media violence, promote positive play, and make good toy choices, the more effective you will be at combating the hazards of media culture. One of the best ways to do this is by creating a community where parents feel comfortable discussing their struggles around media culture issues with each other and developing shared approaches for dealing with entertainment violence issues. For instance, you can talk about what to do for birthday gifts and what television programs are appropriate and inappropriate to watch at each others' houses.[5]

Transforming Imitative War Play into Creative Play: Getting Involved with Superhero and Toy Weapons Play

Here is how Margaret, the preschool teacher who was upset about the disruptive play with guns and superheroes in her classroom, finally dealt with the problem by working with the children as they played:

In desperation, I decided if you can't beat 'em, join 'em! So I tried to get more involved with the play one day when Jules was using a block as a gun and several times had his friends fall down as if they had been shot. I put a block up to my mouth as if it were a walkie-talkie and said, "Calling Officer Jules, Calling Officer Jules. Someone is hurt! We need to get help! We need an officer to help us over here!" At first, Jules kept shooting with great relish saying, "He's the bad guy, he has to be shot. He's bad." I talked into the walkie-talkie, "What did he do to be bad, Officer Jules?" Jules paused, then reported he had robbed a bank. With the walkie-talkie to my mouth, I suggested, "We better get him to jail if he's robbed a bank." By now, as Jules continued shooting, two other children had grabbed blocks as walkie-talkies and reported they were coming to take the robber to jail. Jules came over to join them at the large appliance box in the dramatic play area which quickly was designated "the jail."

Over the next few days, Jules continued to begin his play by pretending to shoot one of his bad guy characters. Each time he asked me to use my walkie-talkie to tell him someone was hurt and needed help. But we also began making props to use in the play: "real" walkie-talkies (out of small pieces of scrap wood that we painted and then attached pieces of electrical wire and nails); a "real" prison (black stripes painted

---

[4] For instance, see: *Children Who See Too Much: Lessons from the Child Witness to Violence Project* by B.M. Groves (Boston: Beacon Press, 2002) and *Children in Danger: Coping with the Effects of Community Violence* by J. Garbarino et al. (San Francisco: Jossey-Bass, 1998).

[5] You can also download from the web, copy, and distribute the Teachers for Resisting Unhealthy Children's Entertainment (TRUCE) "Toy Action Guide" and "Media Violence Action Guide" (See "Resources").

on the box); and a police station outside of the jail with a small table and chair, pretend telephones, note pads, child-made badges, and police hats. This was one of the first times I've seen Jules play in any way but pretend fighting.

Then, independently, a police officer came to visit the school to talk about safety. He was wearing a gun and that led to many of the questions, especially from Jules. As soon as he left, Jules said, "I want to make a gun!" I wasn't sure how to deal with this, but we went to the art table. He asked me to help him draw and cut out a cardboard gun. Other children started making guns too. Then, a child who was just watching us asked, "Margaret, why do you think children like guns so much?" I replied, "What do you think?" After a long silence, Jules murmured, "I think weapons are the strongest things."

The children then asked if I would make a target to shoot their guns at. I made one in the hallway. I got a bit worried as Jules made very loud sound effects as he pretended to shoot at the target and seemed to get very worked up. But the next day, and ever since, there has been markedly less gun play and more creative play involving nonviolent themes.

This teacher uses a wide range of key, developmentally appropriate approaches for facilitating the children's play. While there is much that can be done outside the play in small and large group discussions, she chooses to enter in directly. She uses open-ended questions such as, "What did he do to be bad?" She helps children take specific roles—talking to "Officer Jules." And, she models how to use play materials such as a block as a walkie-talkie and an appliance box as a jail. This approach helps the children (especially Jules) develop a cops and robbers script of their own creation, come up with specific roles to play (police officers and robbers), and use open-ended play materials in creative ways. Her efforts become part of an on-going multi-faceted process, including dealing with new issues involving gun play when the police officer visits the school. We see the rewards that such efforts can bring as Jules seems to become less obsessed with narrowly-scripted gun play and more involved with the kind of creative play that can further his development. He also becomes more closely connected to his teacher as someone who listens and responds to his needs, as witnessed when he feels safe enough to reveal that, 'I think weapons are the strongest things.'

Using a Discussion at Class Meeting to Tame Superheroes

Here is an example of a teacher who used a different approach to transform play that was unsafe, imitative, and narrowly focused on violence into play that could more effectively meet children's needs.

> In the outside play area, several kindergarten children are playing in a large appliance carton covered in aluminum foil. Suddenly, three boys race over and begin to karate chop and kick the box. Just as a teacher comes over to deal with the resulting commotion, a child in the box reaches a fist out and hits one of the "attackers," who bursts into tears crying, "But, I'm a Power Ranger!" [This was the third time in as many days that this teacher has dealt with a crisis created by the presence of the Power Rangers in her classroom.]

> Later in the day, the teacher had a discussion with the children at a class meeting to try to deal with the lack of safety that resulted from the superhero play and to promote creative play that moved beyond the imitative violence. In the conversation, she also encouraged the children to build problem solving and conflict resolution skills. The commentary that accompanies the discussion will help you see how the teacher interpreted and used the children's comments to further the goals of a Peaceable Classroom.

CONVERSATION	COMMENTARY
Teacher: I've noticed a problem, and I need your help figuring out how to solve it. You know how a lot of children have been playing Power Rangers outside lately? [Several children nod in agreement.]	Teacher enlists the whole group of children to work with her on the problem. She helps the children connect the problem to their recent experience with the Power Rangers.
Well, when you play Power Rangers it doesn't feel safe. It seems like almost all they do is run around and fight. And then, it ends up with someone getting upset or hurt—even, crying. Often it's someone who wasn't playing Power Rangers. That's not safe and you know that's the most important rule in our class—feeling safe. What ideas do you have about it?	Without casting blame on the children, she states the problem by explaining the concrete ways children are affected. This helps them make a logical connection between cause and effect. She explains the problem in terms of a classroom rule the children are familiar with—the safety rule. As soon as the problem is explained she brings the children into the discussion.
Jenna: I hate them. I never play.	
T: Yes, I know some of you never play Power Rangers and some of you play a lot. Let's talk about what happens when children who are playing go near those who aren't playing.	The teacher acknowledges Jenna's comment, but also points out the two sides to this problem–both of which are legitimate.

CAMILLA: A fight.

JENNA: I go to a teacher.

RAYMOND: I hit them if they bother me. That stops 'em.

She tries to get the children to elaborate their understanding of the problem.

Young children often focus on the concrete actions and salient aspects of their experiences.

T: Fighting, running to a teacher, and hitting are usually things to do when you don't feel safe. What do the Power Rangers do that doesn't feel safe?

Without making a value judgment, she shows the causal connections between feelings and actions.

She keeps relating children's comments to the basic goal for the classroom to feel safe.

RAYMOND: They messed up the spaceship today.

LAI LING: They're too mean.

T: Can you tell us more about how they are mean?

The teacher tries to get her to focus on the concrete aspects of Power Rangers' behavior to help them see how their actions affect others.

LAI LING: They yell in your face and they kick and punch. I hate them!

T: So you really don't like their noise and their kicking.

She highlights for everyone what it is about the Power Rangers' behavior that creates the problem.

KARLOS: But that's what Power Rangers do. They need to fight.

T: So it sounds like there is a problem. The children playing Power Rangers like to play fight, but other children don't like it when the Power Rangers come near them. It's hard to feel safe when all that fighting and noise is near you and you're trying to do something else. We need to find something to do about the Power Rangers so everyone feels safe. Does anyone have any ideas about how we could do that? You've come up with really good ideas before about how to solve problems like this.

Without expressing a value judgment, she shows how this is a shared problem with two sides. This can help the children get beyond their own egocentric viewpoint.

She again relates the problem to the safety rule, showing exactly what makes the children not feel safe.

Once the problem is clarified, she quickly moves things on to brainstorming possible solutions. She reminds the children that feeling safe is the most important requirement of any solution.

SAMMY: Play somewhere else.

T: You mean Power Rangers play away from other children? [Sammy nods.]

Serving as a translator, she shows how this solution could be put into action.

RIANNAN: Use your words.

T: So what are some of the words you could use?

Again, the teacher brings the focus onto how to make a solution work.

MARK: Say, "Go away."

GILDA: Say, "Don't hit" or "Be quiet."

HENRY: Say, "No play fighting at school"....like at my day care.

KARLOS: Oh, brother. [There are other groans.]

T: Karlos, it sounds like you don't like that idea. Tell us more.

By picking up on his groan, the teacher shows differing viewpoints will be respected. This promotes a sense of autonomy and trust.

KARLOS: They need to fight. That's what they do.

Karlos is comfortable saying what he thinks, rather than what he thinks the teacher wants to hear.

T: I wonder if there are other things that they could do besides fight?

The teacher tries to help the children get beyond their narrow focus on violence by expanding their repertoire of ideas about what the Power Rangers can do. [For more ideas about how to do this, see "Questions To Help Children Work Through Media Violence Issues" at the end of the chapter.]

HUNG MO: They go to high school.

JENNA: They eat in a big room.

DARCY: Hey. The Power Rangers could eat at our restaurant. [Set-up in the dramatic play area.]

This is the kind of unpredictable breakthrough that can come from a group problem-solving session. It transforms a problem into a solution that will expand Power Ranger play beyond just fighting and opens up exciting new possibilities for the play.

T: You've really worked hard on this problem and come up with a lot of good ideas. What if we try some of them tomorrow to see how they work?

The teacher sees fidgeting so she tries to bring closure by choosing two of their solutions that she thinks everyone can agree to and will promote safety.

Power Rangers, what if we choose a special place where you can play outside away from the others? Do you think you could try that? [Several nod.]

And children who play in the restaurant, do you think you can make a meal for the Power Rangers? They must get really hungry. [More nods.]

HUNG MO: But it better be something we like to eat!

T: [She nods and smiles.] You've been sitting for a long time. Let's try these two new ideas. I like that the Rangers will have something to do besides fighting. We'll talk more about how things go and what our restaurant needs to become a cafeteria at our meeting tomorrow. Maybe we can go visit the kitchen here at the school to find out more about what it's like.

As she shows how the two solutions take into account both sides of the problem, she makes sure all the children agree to these solutions.

She also helps them see what they need to do to begin translating both solutions into practice.

Here the teacher states a personal value judgement about fighting.

She ends by making sure the children know they will have a chance to evaluate how their solutions worked after they have tried them.

She plants the seeds for new ideas of how to get more real world information to help further expand the play.

Guidelines for Practice

- **Remember that children do not think about the violence they bring into their play the same way adults do.** For example, Jules focuses on one thing at a time, that the bad guy is bad, without thinking about what makes him bad. Jules also does not worry about the logical causality when he shoots the bad guy dead and then accepts the fact that the bad guy can be locked in jail.

- **Watch children as they play.** Use what you learn as a basis for deciding how to facilitate their play. Look for such information as:

  - What are children's individual play abilities, styles, and interests?

  - What content seems to interest individual children most?

  - What content from the media do children bring into their play? How is it imitative of scripts and how is it creative play of their own design? What kinds of toys seem most and least comfortable and appealing to which children?

  - What kinds of problems come up in the children's play? When do various children run into trouble with their play? With which other children do most of them have conflict?

  - In what areas do children need the most help expanding and developing their play?

- **Help children elaborate the content of their play beyond its narrow focus on violence.** This can be done both in the play (as Margaret does) and out of the play using group discussions and helping the children find more compelling content or scripts to bring into their play. The police officer's visit prompts a whole new direction for the children's play (even though the resulting target practice may not have been the school's intended goal for having him visit).

- **Encourage the use of open-ended and less realistic toys and play materials that can be used in multiple ways.** Margaret uses many such materials in her classroom. Having the appliance box in the classroom provided just the kind of material that was needed at the spur of the moment to help the children turn their shooting play into a more elaborate script. The children also used blocks and then scrounge materials to make their own walkie-talkies, cardboard to make toy guns and a target, and old telephones and small pads for their police station. Here are the kinds of things to keep in mind when choosing play materials for the classroom.

Toy Selection Guidelines[6]

Choose Toys That:	Don't Choose Toys That:
• Can be used in a variety of ways	• Can only be used in one way
• Promote creativity and problem solving	• Encourage everyone to play the same way and work on problems defined by the toy designer
• Can be enjoyed at different ages and developmental stages	• Appeal primarily to a single age or developmental stage
• Will continue to be fun and engaging over time	• Will sit on a shelf after the first 10 minutes
• Can be used with other toys to create new and more complex play opportunities	• Will channel children into imitating the scripts they see on TV
• Promote respectful, non-stereotyped, and nonviolent interactions among children	• Encourage violence and stereotypes that lead to disrespectful, aggressive interactions

- **Develop an approach to media-linked war play that addresses the children's needs as well as your own concerns and goals for the children.** By getting involved with the children's play without condemning it, the teacher opened up a window for helping the children work out issues of violence in their play while feeling safe enough to talk to her about it. Moreover, she furthered her goal of expanding play to a more constructive and less disruptive classroom activity.

- **Work both within and outside of children's play to help them process the violence they see on the screen and to overcome its ill effects.** As the children in Margaret's classroom ended up using her question to Officer Jules to turn the shooting play into police and robber play, we learn something about the children's prior experience with police. It is important to note that none of the children involved seemed to have had direct negative experiences with police, violence, and jails in their lives. Such experiences might have led to different, not totally positive, reactions to the idea of playing with a police theme. As we will discuss in the next chapter, "When the World Is a Dangerous Place," it is very important to stay connected to the children's experiences with entertainment, news, and direct violence when working on these issues both in and out of their play.

    There is much that can be done to help children cope with the lessons about violence that they learn from entertainment media. Chapter 12, "Class Puppets," suggests another means of helping

---

[6]Honey Schnapp and I developed this guide for TRUCE (Teachers Resisting Unhealthy Children's Entertainment). For additional resources on dealing with media violence, war play, and media-linked toys go to the TRUCE web site at www.truceteachers.org.

children expand their understanding of violence through meaningful play. Chapter 13, "Conflict Stories," provides a way for helping children work through ways of solving conflicts in peaceful ways.

- **Outside of play time you can talk to children about the content they are getting from the entertainment violence they bring into their play.** Here are examples of the kinds of questions that can lead to meaningful discussions and help children work through media violence issues:[7]

    You can talk about your reactions to particular programs, characters, and toys—both positive and negative:
    - "What did you think about that show/game?"
    - "I liked it when _____ happened. What did you think about that?"
    - "I didn't like it when _____. I wish they didn't have to hurt each other. What do you think?"
    - "I've noticed that when children play with that media-linked toy, it seems like children often get hurt and upset. Have you noticed that? What do you think we could do to stop that from happening?"

    You can help sort out fantasy from reality.
    - "What was pretend and what was real? How could you tell? What would happen if the characters tried that in real life?
    - "I wonder how they made _____ happen on that show. What do you think? What do you think would happen if children tried to do that in their play?"

    Compare what they saw to their own experience.
    - "Could anything like _____ happen in our lives? When? How would it be the same or different?"
    - "What would you do if you were in that situation?"

    Talk directly about the violence and other mean-spirited behavior children see on the screen.
    - "What do you think about how _____ solved her/his problem. If you had a problem like that what would you do or say?"
    - "Can you think of a way to solve that problem where no one gets hurt and where everyone feels safe?"

    Ask questions that focus on stereotyped images and behaviors:
    - "I wonder why it's always men with big muscles who go to fight? Have you noticed that? What do you think about it?"
    - "It seems like the women always need to get rescued by the men. Have you noticed that? I wonder why? I wonder what else the women could do?"
    - "I wonder why the 'bad guys' have foreign accents? And always wear dark colors?"

- **Provide children with an alternative to the violent content they get from media by suggesting appealing, developmentally appropriate content for their play.** A rich and meaningful curriculum can offer many starting points for play, as can children's direct experiences out of school. But remember that many children will need your help, especially at first, bringing content from their everyday experience into their play. Chapter 14, "Children's Books," offers suggestions for using children's books to provide content that can promote constructive play.

---

[7]Adapted from: *Remote Control Childhood? Combating the Hazards of Media Culture* by D.E. Levin (Washington, DC: National Association for the Education of Young Children, 1998).

8

When the World Is a Dangerous Place: Helping Children Deal with Violence in the News

The Changing World of Childhood

"Officers in Bedford-Stuyvesant shot and killed a man armed with what turned out to be a toy gun yesterday afternoon, the second fatal police shooting in the borough in less than 24 hours, police said."

www.newsday.com/news (August 28, 2002)

On August 29th, 2002, the day after the above story was reported widely in local New York City news, I was in a community near New York City with an economically and racially-diverse group of 4- to 6-year-old children. As they sat down together to eat their snack, a seemingly spontaneous conversation began about what the teacher and I quickly realized was the above news event. The children talked intently with us about the rules they had at home for playing with toy guns, how people might mistakenly think pretend guns were real and vice versa, whether robbers really exist, what robbers actually do, and how to recognize them.

After the children left, the teacher shared her thoughts about what had happened:

I didn't used to think my children were affected much by violence in the news—only by what they saw in movies and on TV programs. Most of the children I work with have parents who seem to be pretty careful about what their children watch.

My thoughts have changed a lot since September 11th. There were children who came in talking about it. They made towers with blocks and used their hands as airplanes to crash into the towers. There were also drawings. I tried to watch what they did and didn't try to stop it. But I wasn't sure what to do other than telling them they were safe at school—that it wouldn't happen to us.

Because September 11th was such a monumental event and since we live near Manhattan, I wasn't surprised that children brought the event to school. But, I figured it would die down and get back to normal... that I wouldn't have to deal much with the news after that. And, after a few months, I got to the point where I pretty much stopped paying attention. Now I'm beginning to notice that bits and pieces of things children hear about in the news do come up, especially in their conversations with each other. Maybe something has changed or maybe I just wasn't paying enough attention before?

And now, look at what happened during snack today, when the children began talking about that story I heard on the local news last night about a man with a toy gun who was shot by police. I didn't realize what they were talking about when they started discussing whether they could play with toy guns. Then, it hit me, "Oh my god—they must be talking about that story from last night!" I was nervous about how to do it, but I'm really glad we had a conversation with them about it.

Teacher of 4-6 year olds, Yonkers, New York, August, 2002

This teacher's reaction to her students, as they unexpectedly began talking about the violence they heard in the news, is similar to stories I have heard repeatedly from teachers and parents of young children. Experiences like this bring us face-to-face with the reality of childhood today—young children hear about violence in the news. It comes from many sources: TV and radio news; talk shows; newspaper headlines and photographs; the internet; 'background' TV monitors in shopping malls, airports, physicians' waiting rooms, or friends' and relatives' houses; as well as in everyday conversation and interactions with siblings and other children. As mass media becomes an increasing presence in children's lives, children cannot help but be exposed to even more violence.

Despite our best efforts to protect children from hearing about violence in the world, we need to accept the fact that for children growing up today, some exposure is inevitable, especially during times of high profile violence in the news like terrorism, war, and school shootings. When they are exposed to news violence, young children often (but not always) will pay attention to it, and consequently, violence can have an impact on their ideas, feelings, and needs.[1] However, when children unexpectedly bring up what they have heard about violent incidents in their conversations, play, or art, many of us are left feeling uncomfortable and unprepared to respond effectively.

Understandably, there are many reasons why most of us would prefer to avoid dealing with these issues as long as possible. We can never be sure what a child might say or where such conversations might lead, and that can be a frightening prospect. We want to protect children from the evils in the world, protect their innocence as long as possible. We worry about saying the wrong thing, something that might add to, rather than alleviate a child's worries. We wish we had a way to make the frightening and disturbing things better—yet we are usually powerless to do so. We worry about how other adults will react to what we do. Never mind the fact that training programs and state certification requirements for teachers of young children rarely address these issues; it often takes time for institutionalized practices to catch up with changing realities.

Whether we are well trained or not, children need our help sorting through what they have heard and figuring out what it means. We have a vital role to play helping them to deal with violence by providing guidance, reassurance, and support. When we play this role, we have the opportunity to influence any problematic lessons they've learned from what they've heard, to help them sort out what is pretend and what is real in the media and in daily life, and to deal with concerns that may arise—particularly surrounding their own safety. We can also help them develop concepts and a language for dealing with what they hear. By getting involved in talking about these issues, we give children assurance that it is okay to talk to the important adults in their lives about the issues that disturb them. When we do not take on this vital task, children are left to deal with the violence on their own.

While recognizing how important it is to address issues related to violence in the news with children is one thing, knowing how to do it is another. For many of you, it will mean traveling down uncharted paths. Yet, I hope that the now familiar principles and practices described throughout this book will provide exactly the kind of foundation you will need to work respectfully and appropriately on these issues with children.

---

[1] As described in Chapter 1, the "continuum of violence" pyramid, the meaning children make of the news violence they hear will depend on their prior experiences along the continuum.

Talking with Children about Violence in the News: A Conversation about Guns and Robbers

Talking directly with young children about news events is one of several effective approaches for meeting children's need to work through what they hear in the news. We can learn a lot about how to begin the conversation from the teacher who realized that her children were discussing a shooting that had been on the news the previous night. In the midst of her surprise and uncertainty, her spontaneous responses grappled with several of the complexities involved in trying to address children's needs around violence in the news. The commentary accompanying the text highlights some of the key issues involved.

Here's the conversation the teacher had with the children about the shooting.

CONVERSATION	COMMENTARY
JOSEF: You can only play with water guns—not toy guns—because a robber could go in the toy store with a real gun and put it with the toy guns. You would take it thinking it was a toy gun and you could shoot someone with it.	Josef seems to be trying to work something out about pretend versus real guns. This comment confuses the teacher until she realizes Josef heard about the shooting of a robber with a toy gun. By raising the issue this way, Josef shows that it is on his mind and that he feels safe raising it with his teacher. Children quickly learn where they can and cannot talk about these things and Josef may be testing out the water here.
TEACHER: So you think a robber could go in a toy store?	Confused by this seemingly strange comment and not yet sure why the issue of toy and real guns came up, she simply reflects back one key aspect of his comment. This kind of response, called active listening, lets him know she is interested and it is okay to talk about it.
HENRY: [turning to teacher] Are there really robbers?	Henry is looking for factual information (but not necessarily an adult definition). He may be trying to sort out pretend from real and feels comfortable talking to the adult about it.
T: What have you heard about robbers?	Before answering, the teacher focuses on finding out more about what Henry knows and may want to know. Again, this conveys that it is okay to ask the question and she is interested in his ideas. Asking for more information is usually the best way to start a discussion about potentially scary or disturbing news events. It helps us decide how to respond in a way that addresses children's understanding and needs.

MARGARET: They take things like money and jewelry.

Children often do a good job responding on their own to each other's questions and concerns. They often focus on concrete and visible aspects of things.

RANDY: Is that what a robber does?

KEVIN: They have guns. They can really shoot them.

Guns are clearly on several children's minds; the teacher begins to wonder if something special has led to this interest coming up today.

MARGY: Only real guns can shoot, not toy guns. That's why there are water guns for children. I can have them.

This shows her effort to sort out fantasy from reality. She also is connecting what she knows about guns to herself and her own safety. Children usually relate news information to themselves.

T: Yes. Grown-ups work hard to make sure that children don't get hurt by real guns or by robbers.

The teacher is now wondering if some children have heard about the robber with the toy gun. Whether they have or have not, she conveys that it is the job of trusted adults to make decisions and rules that ensure children's safety.

RANDY: [Hesitantly] When someone takes a child, is that a robber?

Randy seems unsure about asking this question. He may be raising it because he's heard about the high profile child abduction murders that were in the news throughout the summer.

T: Taking a child? Have you heard something about that?

The teacher, being careful about not jumping to any erroneous conclusions, wants to know more about what he knows.

MARGARET: Yes. A robber is anyone who takes anything, even children.

Margaret knows a lot and is quite sure about her concept of a robber. She seems to enjoy sharing what she knows with the other children.

T: There aren't a lot of robbers—hardly any. I've never known a robber!

The teacher, sensing that the children have a lot of information and feelings about robbers, focuses on the safety issue. Since children only focus on the fact of the robber, they need help with the reality that there aren't robbers everywhere and that they are safe.

BRAD: [Excitedly] I didn't either. Neither did my mother or father!

Clearly, Brad and others relate meaningfully (and perhaps with relief) to the teacher's reassurance.

SHIRLEY: Mine didn't either!

KEVIN: Well if you saw a robber you'd know anyway. You can always recognize a robber!

Kevin has his own way of helping himself feel safe—being able to recognize robbers so he knows if he is in danger.

T: So you would know if you saw a robber? Tell us how you know a robber?

Again, the teacher explores what a child's comments mean to the child before responding.

KEVIN: He wears a black shirt and black pants, and black shoes and a black hat.

It is common for young children to try to figure out how to recognize "bad guys." They often do this by focusing on the salient, concrete aspects that they can see—i.e., what robbers wear. This can lead to incorrect conclusions and stereotyped ideas. This illogic can lead children to answers that help them feel safe—or, at other times, scared.

T: So you would know if you saw a robber because he would wear black?

[A couple of children say yes.]

The teacher clarifies and reflects back what Kevin said. This active listening response helps all children follow what is going on and can lead more children to make comments. The teacher does not correct Kevin. Providing correct adult information often is not what children are asking for when they discuss news. This teacher takes the lead from Kevin. There are times, however, when giving a little bit of correct information can clear up misconceptions that scare and upset children, help them feel safe, and influence the lessons they learn.

T: So you know a lot about robbers. How did you learn about them?

Now that she thinks the children are having this discussion because they heard a news story, she asks an open-ended question to try to find out if her conclusion is correct.

KEVIN: At school [kindergarten]. We saw a movie. It told us about robbers.

He seems to have had some sort of safety program at his school. His conclusion, that robbers wear black, may have been an unintended outcome of that program. That's why it is so important to have ongoing discussions.

KEVIN: On TV.

Television is a major source of children's exposure to both entertainment and real world violence.

RANDY: I had a dream about a robber that had a toy gun that looked like a real gun—no one knew it was pretend.

Randy returns to ideas related to the previous night's news story that he seems to have heard. He focuses on the logic of what happened—thinking a pretend gun was real. Scary things children see and hear can affect their sleep and dreams.

T: So you had a dream about a toy gun? When was that?

The teacher acknowledges what he said and then asks a question about when the dream occurred to establish its probable connection with the news story.

RANDY: Last night. I slept with my mom!

Volunteering that he went to his mom's bed implies that he felt scared by the dream, but had a way to help him feel safe.

T: Dreams can be pretty scary. It sounds like sleeping with your mom helped. That's good you had something you could do to make it less scary.

The teacher raises the scary aspect of his dream, and so conveys to all the children that it is okay to raise scary topics. She focuses on the importance of finding things to do to feel safe when you are scared.

MARGARET: That really happened, you know. He got shot with a real gun. [Other children nod in agreement.]

JOSEF: Yeah. He had a toy gun but it looked real.

It is Margaret who finally brings the previous night's news story directly into the discussion. As others nod and Josef pipes in with more of the story the children seem ready to discuss it directly. While the teacher might have brought it up if the children did not, it often takes time for the children to work up to talking about the story directly.

BRAD: No. Robbers don't have toy guns!

KEVIN: Yes he did!

Some children are exposed to more news than others. Brad seems to be reacting to what the children said without knowledge of the news story. One difficult challenge for adults when discussing news with a group is helping those children who know about a story work it out while at the same time trying not to scare or upset those who do not know about it.

T: So you heard something in the news about someone—a robber—that got hurt with a real gun or a toy gun?

The teacher asks a question to clarify for all the children the news story that is being discussed. She focuses on real versus toy guns which seems to be what is confusing the children and what they are trying to figure out.

JOSEF: No. He got hurt with a toy gun. That's why you can't play with toy guns. Only water guns.

Josef uses the news story to justify the rule he has about only using water guns and not "toy" guns. Clearly this is an important issue for him, because he began the whole class discussion with a similar comment—but when he says it now, it makes more sense to the adult. Children often relate what they hear about in the wider world to themselves—using what they know, what they do, or what they have experienced directly to help them understand it.

HENRY: [Proudly] I have a "....." water gun. It shoots really far. My mom got it for me.

Seemingly triggered by Josef's comment about playing with water guns, Henry's comment ignores the news story and focuses on the special water gun his mom got him. Young children often do this kind of chaining. They focus on one aspect of what they hear—the part that is most interesting or meaningful to them—losing sight of the main topic.

T: So some of you can play with water guns not toy guns because your moms and dads think they're safer. Guns can be scary and hurt people. Grow-ups work hard to make sure guns can't hurt you.

The teacher does not correct Henry. She tries to summarize the key elements the children raised that are most connected to their own experiences. She ends by focusing on how adults make decisions that are aimed at keeping them safe. This is most often what young children need to know when they have heard or talked about something that can make the world seem like a dangerous place. This kind of discussion can actually help parents in their efforts to set limits on their children's use of toy guns.

[Several children nod and say, "My parents too."]

The children seem to like to hear that their parents are taking care of them and keeping them safe.

This conversation illustrates many of the key elements that are important to keep in mind when talking with children about the violence they hear in the news. The teacher's responses convey a sense that it is safe to raise an issue they heard in the news, and that she is there to help them sort it out. She accomplishes this by:

- listening carefully to what the children have to say and asking open-ended questions in order to learn more about what they think and know;

- responding to the issues the children raise and seem to be concerned about rather than bringing in her own agenda or trying to provide "correct" answers or "teach" a lot of factual information;

- providing the information and support she thinks the children need to feel safe; and,

- seeing this discussion as part of an on-going process whereby she saves for later discussions some of the issues the children raise; for instance, she holds off helping the children fully work out their confusion about toy versus real guns as well as Kevin's stereotyped idea about robbers wearing black.[2]

---

[2]The information in Chapter 6, "Anti-bias Education," will help you figure out ways to deal with this kind of stereotypical thinking when it comes up.

The children's comments reveal a great deal about how they make sense of violence they hear about in the news, how their level of development influences this meaning-making process, and the needs that arise as a result. For instance:

- We see that the children feel safe enough to raise the issue. Moreover, they seem to welcome the opportunity to talk about what they have heard and what they think about it, as well as to ask and answer each others' questions.

- The children each relate what they heard to what is important to themselves and what they already know (which is different for each child)—for instance, whether or not they can use toy guns and why.

- They are not all interested in the same issues, though: some focus more on toy versus real guns, while others want to talk about robbers.

- Children tend to keep their focus on one thing at a time (as opposed to seeing the whole picture), and generally it is on the most salient aspects of what they heard—guns and robbers. Usually, they do not pay much attention to the underlying causality or reasons why the situation occurred.

- Also, children use differing levels of logic in interpreting what they heard—for instance, one child seems to have a logical concept of robber (anyone who takes anything), whereas another child looks at what robbers do on a case-by-case basis.

Beyond Talk: Using Play and Art to Work Out Ideas about Violence in the News

No matter how many meaningful conversations we have with children about violence in the news, most young children will still need other, more concrete ways to express and work through violence issues than words alone can provide. As we have seen in earlier chapters of this book, dramatic play and art are generally the most powerful avenues available to young children for working out an understanding of their experience. Play and art also provide adults with the crucial information we need to develop strategies for meeting children's needs. For these reasons, it is very important to provide children with a variety of creative forums for expressing and working through the ideas of violence they have heard about in the news. The following examples of adults' efforts to do this powerfully illustrate how to put into practice the guidelines outlined at the end of this chapter for helping children deal with violence they have encountered in the media.

September 11th Drawings

Soon after the September 11th tragedy, a parent shared with me the following drawing that her four-year-old son, Sam, had made of the World Trade Center. (See Figure 8.1)

When she asked him to tell her about his drawing, Sam talked about "the building that fell down" [on the left] and the "sooooooo big airplane wing" [along the top of the page]. Then he pointed to the "people" he drew outside the building and said, "These are the people on the swings. When the building fell down no one was hurt, because all the people were outside playing!" The mother was taken

Figure 8.1: Four-year-old Sam's World Trade Center drawing with people outside playing on swings "so they didn't get hurt."

off guard by Sam's apparent failure to recognize what had really happened at the World Trade Center. At the same time, she did not try to correct him. She respected his need to make his own meaning of the event, especially because he seemed very satisfied with his drawing and interpretation of the event. When I saw the drawing, I asked the mother if she had any idea why Sam had chosen to bring swings into the picture. She thought for a moment, and then her eyes lit up as she said, "My goodness, he had just learned to swing by himself and was very excited about it!" Sam brought in something that was very much on his mind at the time of the tragedy, his new mastery of swinging. This provided him with a way to feel powerful, strong, and invulnerable. Unlike Louisa, who ran under a tree when she saw an airplane, Sam seems to have used his four-year-old level of thinking (which is very different from the logic of an adult) to create an interpretation of the event which did not require dealing with the terrible death and destruction. Young children's way of thinking may contribute to logical and illogical fears about the violence they hear; the same kind of thinking can also allow them to make conclusions that help them feel safe.

Many teachers have described drawings of the World Trade Center that children made after September 11th. Although most of these drawings were immediately recognizable and looked very similar to one another, when we look more closely, we usually discover that they are not as similar as they first appear. As we can see from Sam's drawing, a lot can be discovered about individual children's needs and developmental understanding when we take a closer look at the things they create. Sam created his own unique meanings based on: his current level of development, his prior experience, and

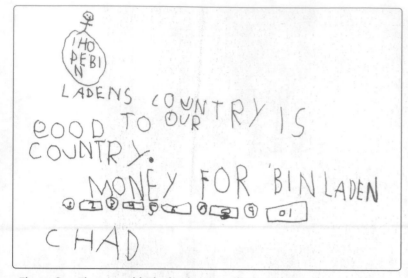

Figure 8.2: Five-year-old Chad's drawing of "Money for Bin Ladden" suggests that Bin Laden "buy some nails and wood to make a house" so he doesn't have to sleep on rocks in a cave.

what was most important to him at the time. Having an opportunity to draw allowed him to work out this interpretation and reassure his mother that she did not need to provide any additional information at that time.

In another, more unusual example of a child's effort to sort out what he heard about September 11th and its aftermath, Chad, a kindergartner, made this drawing about Osama Bin Laden. (See Figure 8.2) He wrote on the drawing, "I hope Bin Laden's country is good to our country." He then wrote the words "money for Bin Laden," and drew a picture to illustrate. As is so important when working with children on issues like these, I wanted to find out more about what Chad was trying to convey in his drawing. So I requested that his mother ask Chad an open-ended question about why he

wanted to give Bin Laden money. When she did, he replied, "So he can buy some nails and sticks and build himself a house. Then he won't have to live in a cave and he'll be nice to our country!"

Chad's response shows that he has heard something about Bin Laden's alleged role in the September 11th tragedy. He seems to have attached special meaning to the idea that Bin Laden lives in a cave. In the weeks after Chad made this comment, I heard several other children mention caves. I asked them what they knew about caves, most replied that they "saw a cave in the Disney movie, 'Lion King' and it was a place where wild animals live." As discussed in Chapter 1, when we look at the continuum of violence in children's lives, children often use what they have learned from violence in entertainment media to interpret things they hear about in the news. In the case of caves, children learned from a movie that caves were scary places where you would not want to live.

Following from this, it seems possible that Chad might have decided that Bin Laden was "mean" or "bad" because he did not like living in a scary cave, and if he had enough money to build a house, then he would not be mean or bad. When children hear about violence in the news, they often try to work out an understanding of the bad guys—how you can recognize them and what makes them bad. We saw this in the discussion about toy guns and robbers when Kevin said robbers could always be recognized by the black clothes they wear.

One very encouraging aspect of Chad's drawing is that, despite the fact that a majority of the responses that were being discussed in the news focused on violent retaliation, he was looking for a nonviolent, concrete way to "make things better." When children hear about a disturbing event, they often look for concrete ways to try to improve the situation—to try to make a positive difference. While it is important for young children to know that it is the responsibility of adults to keep children safe and create peace in the world, Peaceable Classrooms can actively help children find developmentally appropriate, non-violent ways to feel like they are making a difference. The final section of this chapter offers some suggestions for ways to begin.

Figure 8.3: After the tragedy of September 11th, adults all over the world reported children building and knocking down block towers; these children added injured miniature people and a fire truck to help the injured.

Figure 8.4: Soon after the bombing of the Federal Courthouse in Oklahoma City, these children spontaneously began using dramatic play in the block area to work out an understanding of what they had heard, including about the people who died.

Figure 8.5: Several months after 9/11, these boys spent a week "rebuilding" a very elaborate and fully recovered New York City. Children often use their play, art, and writing to transform violent events into more peaceful ones.

September 11th Play

In addition to drawing pictures, most children also use pretend play to work out an understanding of what they hear in the news. Almost immediately after September 11th, parents and teachers reported children making tall block buildings and crashing them down with accompanying sound effects. (See Figure 8.3) There were variations in how children did this. Some put miniature play people in their buildings who were buried under the falling blocks. Some tried to bury themselves under the falling blocks and pretend to be dead. Still others used small construction materials like Legos to build tall towers that could easily fall apart. Since children's efforts to work things out often focus on the most salient and dramatic aspects of an event, it is not surprising that so much of the block building play that adults described sounded remarkably similar, centering around the most vivid images of the event: tall buildings, crashing planes, and buried people.

This kind of block play is very similar to teacher accounts of block play during other terrorist attacks on buildings, for instance, after the terrorist bombing of the courthouse in Oklahoma City in 1995. (See Figure 8.4)

In both of the examples above, the children's play gradually changed over time from being more violent and scary to being more peaceful and safe. Just as Sam and Chad's thinking made it possible for them to use their drawing to come up with scenarios that created a safe world, so can children's play help them construct a sense of safety. This is what happened in the two examples of block play described above. The World Trade Center block play turned into children pretending to be rescue workers who put out the fires, and the Oklahoma City block play became doctors taking injured people to the hospital. This happened with the help of teachers who provided firefighter and medical equipment at opportune moments in the play. Bringing in content and materials that are familiar, concrete, and readily translatable into dramatic play often can help children move their play with violence to a more peaceful resolution. For example, children outside New York City transformed their collapsed building block play into a rebuilt and safe New York City. (See Figure 8.5) In evaluating how well play is meeting a child's need to work out violence issues, you can look for and try to promote this kind of transformation over time. The suggestions for facilitating play in Chapter 7 will also help you in this effort.

Guidelines for Practice: Helping Children Use Play to Work Out Violent and Disturbing Content[3]

- Watch children as they play to learn more about what they know, what worries them, and what they are struggling to understand.

- Remember that for many children it is normal and helpful to bring into their play graphic aspects of what they have seen and heard.

- If the play gets scary or dangerous, gently intervene and redirect it. For example, ask children, "How could people help each other?" Or provide toys such as rescue vehicles and medical equipment.

- Help them come up with ways for extending the play. Try to follow the children's lead in the roles that you take rather than taking over.

- After the play, talk to children about what they played. Reassure their safety. Answer questions simply. Clear up confusions.

- Try to teach alternatives to the harmful lessons children may be learning from the violence they bring to their play.

When Pretend Play Meets the Real World

Shortly before the first anniversary of September 11th, as news of war with Iraq was rapidly escalating (and after a summer of news reports of several children being kidnapped), the mother of six-year-old Andrew contacted me by e-mail. Until recently, she and her husband had successfully protected him from any apparent interest in gunplay (as well as from exposure to violence in entertainment and news media), but now he had become quite involved in gunplay with children in his neighborhood. She wondered why it might have developed now and whether she should be concerned.

I quickly realized that since children use play to work through confusing events, it is perfectly reasonable to expect to see more war play in children as the world around them becomes more and more saturated with news about war, terrorism, and violence. We have already seen that parents cannot fully

---

[3]Adapted from the 2002-2003 *Truce Toy Action Guide* (www.truceteachers.org).

protect their children from the onslaught. So I tried to reassure the mother about the potential importance of Andrew's play and suggested she use the guidelines listed above for "Helping Children Use Play to Work out Violent and Scary Content." About a week later, I received the following reply:

> Things have calmed down since I first wrote. I think it's because we changed our approach. Now, instead of saying, "No guns," we say, "WHY are you using guns?" This leads to further discussion about the theme.
>
> Andrew actually started talking about bad guys and how "it could happen anytime, Mom!" When questioned further, he explained that "they" could come into our house at any time and take our stuff (apparently his biggest fear at present). He had fantasies of how they might get into the house (through his second floor window, without figuring they'd need a ladder)... and while I know he's probably more fearful given his recent foray into the real world via first grade, this seems to have been a persistent theme. I tried to reason with him that our two dogs would keep him safe at all costs. Still, he held on to his fear. (There has been much talk about war and several abductions around here including one suspicious man in our neighborhood six months ago, which I know the kids are talking about, so our son does probably have daily reminders.)
>
> There is one thing that really did work. A friend, who was living in Japan, brought us back a pair of gargoyles that the Japanese put on either side of the front door to protect their homes. I figured I'd try bringing them out and sharing the folklore with Andrew. We ended up putting them outside his and his sister's bedrooms on the floor next to their doors. The very next morning Andrew entered our room and said with a smile "It worked!" and he's slept well every night since then.

This mother's account illustrates how powerful it can be when we connect with children around their efforts to deal with violence, including toy gunplay. It can help them:

- use their play to meet their needs around issues of violence

- sort out pretend from real violence

- clear up misconceptions

- find meaningful ways (that do not always follow adult logic) to feel safe and secure

- learn that they can go to trusted adults for reassurance and assistance when they are puzzled or scared, and that what they say will be respected.

Approaches for Raising News Violence Issues with Children

As we have seen from the examples so far in this chapter, there are few formulae for deciding when and how to bring up events in the news with children. Sometimes, as illustrated by the conversation at the beginning of this chapter, the teacher only needs to figure out how to respond, because the children raise an issue themselves. The examples of children bringing news violence issues into their drawings and play provide another kind of direct entry into raising the issue with children. However, it is important to keep in mind that children do not always directly or immediately raise news topics they have heard about in their conversations or hands-on activities. Here are some suggestions of other ways you can begin working with children on news violence issues.

- **Sometimes, an unforeseen event triggers a response in children to something they have heard about in the news.** For instance, one parent who lived in New Hampshire described driving to Boston with her five-year-old son about a month after September 11th. She thought he did not know about September 11th and she had never discussed it with him. Suddenly, he pointed to the first very tall building they drove by and excitedly said, "Look Mommy! They've already rebuilt the World Trade Center." Somewhat stunned, the mother responded, "You heard about the World Trade Center?" Incredulous, her son said, "You mean you didn't hear about it, Mommy!" Once both mother and child had calmed down, this initial encounter with a skyscraper opened up the channels for a meaningful give-and-take discussion to begin.

- **Often, we have to be on our toes to recognize peculiar behavior that reveals that a child is thinking about the news.** In one poignant example, a parent told me about the following experience. About three weeks after September 11th, her three-year-old daughter, Sophia, was outside playing at her childcare center when an airplane flew overhead. The teacher noticed that Sofia ran and hid under a bush as the plane passed over. Later, the teacher told the mother about what had happened and asked if Sofia knew about the terrorist attack. The mother replied that she did not think so because her family had been careful not to watch the news when Sofia was around. Going home in the car that day, she asked Sofia, "Have you heard about anything that happened in a place called New York City (they lived in New York State)?" To her amazement and surprise, Sofia responded, "Yes, Mommy, I heard about some 'bad men' who knocked a building down with an airplane." She then asked, "Sofia, when you have been waking up at night and coming to our bedroom [something that had been happening a lot lately and which the mother thought was related to Sofia having just begun going to childcare], were you ever thinking about that airplane?" Sofia replied, "Yes, Mommy, and maybe those bad guys will come and hit me!" The mother then reassured Sofia that no planes had ever crashed into a building in their town and that the airport people were working hard to make sure no more "bad men" could get on a plane again.

  Clearly, Sofia knew more than her mother ever imagined possible. But once alerted by the teacher that September 11th might be an issue for Sofia, the mother opened up exactly the kind of give-and-take discussion children need to have with adults around issues surrounding violence in the news. She raised the issue directly by trying to find out what Sofia knew. She then based her responses on what Sofia said, tried to connect it to Sofia's current behavior, and worked to help her feel safe. Before jumping to any conclusions about why the airplane sent Sofia running under the bush or immediately opening up the subject directly with Sofia herself, the teacher went to the mother to try to find out more about what Sofia, who was only three, knew about September 11th. This helped Sofia and her mother connect with each other—in a positive way—around an issue that was having an impact on Sofia.

- **Sometimes, you can get a sense from children that they need to talk about something in the news; in this situation, it will be helpful to raise the issue directly with the children.** This point was dramatically brought home to me around the time of the first anniversary of the September 11th events. I was visiting a classroom where children were building and knocking down tall block towers. The teacher asked the children to tell her about their buildings and why they were knocking them over. The children said, "Oh, they're just buildings that fall over." Probe questions from the teacher did not move the conversations any further. Then, at the early morning meeting on Sept. 11th, the teacher subtly, yet directly raised the issue of the anniversary with the children by asking, "Has anyone heard anything about today being a special day?" Several hands enthusiastically went up, and all but one answer about the anniversary. After the meeting, the children again built high block towers that they knocked down. This time when the teacher went over to discuss what was happening, the children labeled the towers the World Trade Center and the Empire State Building.

- **You can create regular and predictable avenues for raising questions with children about the news and any violence issues they want to discuss.** One approach several teachers have told me works quite well, especially with older children, is creating a regular time (such as once a week at the regular class meeting) for discussing the news. One effective way to start such a discussion is by asking the children, "Has anyone heard about anything in the news they would like to talk about?" This can be difficult at first—you will never be sure what issues will come up. It can take a while for children to learn that it is safe to raise the issues they are concerned about and to develop the language they need for talking about what they know. Much of the time they are likely to raise stories about such topics as sports events, the weather, and stories from their families (which are all of value, too). This is because young children's ideas about the "news" often center on themselves and rarely focus on one narrow topic. When more serious topics do come up, try to use the same give-and-take approach for leading discussions illustrated throughout this book.

- **As children get more comfortable and skillful talking about the news, you can also intentionally develop a more extensive "News" curriculum project.** As described above, much of the news covered will not be about news violence. One first grade classroom began working on such a project in the fall of 2002, as I was in the process of revising this book. It was introduced to the class on the second day of school. The teachers began by telling the children that the class was going to do a project during the year on "the news." Each week, they would write "news stories" to share with the class. A conversation ensued about what the children knew about the news. They came up with examples of several kinds of news that focused primarily on themselves and their own personal experiences—news about pets, summer activities, sports events, the weather.

  The children's first news reports focused exclusively on stories about themselves—about pets, walking to school, family visitors. When they were done sharing their stories, the teacher told her news story: "She was excited because she had just received an e-mail from a friend who was in a country named Bahrain. It was very far away in a place called the Middle East. Immediately two children raised their hand and said they had heard of the Middle East. When the teacher asked them what they had heard one child responded he had heard of Afghanistan and he thought that might be in the Middle East. Suddenly, several hands quickly shot up in the air and children began making such comments as: "I heard that the people who bombed the World Trade Center came from Afghanistan." "I know someone who used to work in a building next to the one the plane hit." "I think the terrorists must have worn costumes so no one could recognize them." "I went to the World Trade Center when I was five years old." The floodgates had opened—and once they did, almost all the children knew things they enthusiastically wanted to share.

  Over the next few days, there were several meetings in which the children could continue to discuss the issues that now seemed to be of such pressing concern to them. Gradually the teachers began to answer the children's questions, help them clarify their thinking, and clear up misconceptions. As the children returned to their regular news reports over the next few weeks, they covered a wide range of topics, from personal developments to events in the news, including discussions about the war.

Learning to Care and to Make a Difference in the World[4]

Too often, the lesson children learn from what they hear in the news is that the wider world is a violent and scary place where people do terrible things to each other. It is important that we also try to be on the look out for news stories to share with children about positive things that happen—after September 11th there were many examples in the news of people helping each other in both big and small ways. Such stories can help children see that there are many people across the globe who are working to create a caring and peaceful world, and that there are actions one can take to help make things better.

In addition to hearing about positive events in the world, it is also important for children to come up with their own ideas about what might help solve the problems they hear about. We see this happening when Chad wanted to give money to Bin Laden to build a house (so he wouldn't have to live in a cave). Children can also come up with actions to take that will lessen someone's hardship or suffering. This happens when children write letters of concern and support to people who have been harmed by a crisis or tragedy, or to a community leader or politician about their ideas for how some problem should be resolved. It also happens when they try to collect money to help others who are in need. Remember that as children take these actions. The specific impact of their actions should not be their focus. What is most important is that they learn they can help.

Guidelines for Practice: Helping Children Learn to Care and Take Action

- Make sure children know it is the job of adults to make the world a safe place for children, even though children can contribute. Children should not think that their own sense of safety and well-being is dependent on their own actions.

- As children plan actions to take, do not expect them to plan the most effective possible actions from the adult point of view. They cannot fully think through the logic of their ideas. As long as safety is assured, children need to try their ideas out for themselves to see how they work.

- Choose topics for action where children are likely to experience some kind of direct effect of their actions. For instance, it is often more meaningful for children to do something around issues that directly affect their lives or from which they get a direct response.

- Choose topics for action with which you are comfortable sharing your power and control with children. While your input is vital to the children's successful actions, the children will probably come up with action plans that are different from the ones you would use if it were up to you.

Working with Parents

However you approach helping children deal with what they hear in the news, try to keep parents informed about your efforts. Seek their advice regarding their children's experiences and needs, help them better understand the issues at hand, and work to meet their children's needs in regards to these issues. When the teachers mentioned above decided to develop a news curriculum project for their first grade class, they recognized the importance of involving the parents as much as possible. However,

---

[4]For a more detailed discussion about how to help children learn to take action see Chapter 8, "Helping Children Take Action" in *Remote Control Childhood* by D. E. Levin (Washington, DC: National Association for the Education of Young Children, 1998) and *That's Not Fair! A Teacher's Guide to Activism with Young Children* by A. Pelo and F. Davidson (St. Paul, MN: Redleaf Press, 2000).

they also realized that some parents would probably be uncomfortable at the prospect of having their children exposed to disturbing world events. Here is how the teachers introduced the news project to parents in the first weekly newsletter they sent home. The teachers invited parents to sit in on weekly news meetings and sent home materials to help parents talk about news issues that came up with their children. They continued to report regularly on the project in subsequent newsletters.

Dear Families,

We've just completed our first full week of school! It's been a busy week of learning new routines and getting used to the longer days of first grade. Before starting our weekly Tuesday morning writing and discussion sessions about children's news, we began by asking for the children's ideas about what news is. We were not surprised that what they focused on was primarily things in their own lives, for example: birthdays, events from home, pets, sports, weather, entertainment, and travel. On Tuesday morning the children drew and wrote on individual pieces of paper their news for the week. As the children shared we noted all the different categories news can fit into. Megan shared that letters and email can also be news. She explained that she had just received an email message from a friend in a country called Bahrain in the Middle East. We looked for Bahrain on a map. Mention of the "Middle East" led to a flurry of hands, indicating all the children who wanted to talk. One child said that Afghanistan is in the Middle East. This became the springboard for many children to chime in with their ideas about current events relating to Afghanistan and then back to September 11th. The children were very animated and engaged in the discussion. We promised we would continue the discussion the following day so that children could further express their ideas. On Wednesday morning the children had much more to say. One child stated that, "I think the terrorists were from Afghanistan. The people either went to jail or died. The state police fly in the air and shoot." Through this discussion it became evident that some of the children had a variety of misconceptions about the destruction of the Twin Towers and the war in Afghanistan. Some of these included terrorists parachuting from the planes, taking gliders to safety, and escaping through the tail of the plane. We mostly listened to what the children had to say—making sure they felt safe and comfortable talking in the group. We sought more information from the children about their ideas and clarified for them that there are confusing issues. These are anxious times and we want the children to feel comfortable enough to continue to process what they hear in the news. This will be a topic discussed at curriculum night.

To the teachers' satisfaction, the following letter was unexpectedly delivered to the classroom by a parent soon after the first class newsletter reporting on the project went home.

Dear Teachers,

I wanted to thank you for the note sent home Friday. I now feel like I have a good sense of what's going on in the classroom. Every time I entered it seemed to be bustling with actvity. My growing curioisty is now satisfied.

I also need to thank you for inviting the children into an open forum for discussing their understanding of September 11th, 2001 and the events or feelings related to it. We sheltered our daughter by banning all television coverage and most radio broadcast related to the tragedy. We felt this was best since her father is a firefighter, and so many children like her were orphaned. She has lost three great-grandparents in her lifetime, one she was very fond of, and pretty much associates death with old age. However, funerals have prompted her to ask us when we are going to die.

Because of her worries about death, her father's profession, and an upcoming trip we had planned involving two plane rides, we only talked about it when questioned. The questions were few and centered around planes crashing; war was never discussed.

Our daughter's grandparents and a few uncles and aunts are Afrian-American Muslims. I was very worried about the backlash against Muslims in America after Spetember 11th. I appreciate you pointing out to the children that the terrorists did not represent one race or nationality.

Summary of Guidelines for Practice

- **Protect children, especially young children, as much as possible from exposure to news violence on the TV, radio, or in adults' conversations.** While it is rarely possible to protect them fully from news violence, having safety and security predominate is still vital for healthy development. Therefore, the more you can limit exposure to media violence the better. The more news violence they see, the more likely they are to think that the world is dangerous, and the more likely they will need help undertanding the violent content they see.

- **Trusted adults have a vital role to play in helping children feel safe and sort out what they see and hear.** When exposed to violence, children need to know you are there to help them in an ongoing way and that they won't be criticized for bringing up the issue or saying what they really think. How you react plays a big role in determining how they think and feel, as well as what they learn.

- **Take your lead from what the children do and what you know about them as individuals.** Base your responses on the age, prior experiences, specific needs, and unique concerns of individual children.

  - **Young children will not understand violence as adults do.** When they see or hear about something frightening, they often relate it to themselves and worry about their own safety. They tend to focus on one thing at a time and the most salient aspects of what they see. Because they haven't yet developed logical causal thinking, it is hard for them to figure out the logic of what happened and why, or sort out what is pretend and what is real. They relate what they hear to themselves, to what is important to them, as well as to what they already know. This can lead to many misunderstandings: "Mommy works in a skyscraper; it can blow up too!" or "Planes in the war carry bombs; so planes I see in the sky carry bombs too!"

  - **With age, children begin to think more about what underlies an event and to consider possible real world implications.** They use more accurate language and make logical causal connections, but still do not understand all the meanings and, consequently, can develop misunderstandings and fears. Find out the meanings behind what they say, and base your responses on what they seem to know and be asking.

- **Start by finding out what children know.** If a child brings up a violent event in conversation, you might ask, "What have you heard about that?" You can start a conversation with, "Have you heard anything about a plane crash [or bombs]? What did you hear?"

- **Answer questions and clear up misconceptions that worry or confuse.** You don't need to provide the full story. Just tell children what they seem to want to know. Don't worry about giving right answers or clearing up ideas that don't agree with yours. You can help them learn to distinguish real from pretend violence. You can calmly voice your feelings and concerns to reassure them about their safety.

- **Support children's efforts to use play, art, and writing to work out an understanding of scary things they see and hear.** It's normal for children to do this in an ongoing way. It helps them work out ideas and feelings, and it demonstrates what they know and what worries them. Open-ended (versus highly-structured) play materials—blocks, airplanes, emergency vehicles, miniature people, a doctor's kit, markers and paper—help children with this.

- **Be on the lookout for signs of stress.** Changes in behavior such as increased aggression or withdrawal, difficulty separating from parents or sleeping, or troubles with transition are all signs that additional support is needed. Protecting children from violent media images, maintaining routines, providing reassurance and extra hugs can help children regain equilibrium.

- **Help children learn alternatives to the harmful lessons they may be learning about violence and prejudice.** Talk about nonviolent ways to solve conflicts in their own lives. Help them look at different points of view in conflicts. Point to positive experiences with people who are different from themselves. Try to complicate their thinking rather than tell them how to think.

- **Discuss what adults are doing to make the situation better and what children can do to help.** Children can feel secure when they see adults working to keep the world safe. Taking meaningful steps themselves can also help children feel more in control.

- **Have regular conversations with parents and other professionals.** Work together to support each other's efforts to create a safe environment for children. This includes sharing information that comes up with particular children, developing effective response strategies together, and agreeing to protect children from unnecessary exposure to violence. Talking together can also help adults meet their own personal needs in dealing with the violence that surrounds us.

Part Three

Starting Points for Curriculum Development in Peaceable Classrooms

As we have seen, effective Peaceable Classrooms grow out of our understanding of how children develop ideas about peace, conflict, and violence and our knowing how to infuse this knowledge into the curriculum and daily classroom life. Once you have this developmental framework, you can begin to look at specific curriculum activities and make informed judgments about how they might contribute to your Peaceable Classroom.

In my work with teachers, I have seen many highly original and effective examples of Peaceable Classrooms. The richest approaches generally provide enough structure for children to organize their ideas and actions, but are flexible and open enough so that what happens can evolve and change with you and your children.

In the chapters that follow, I have included a few of the most exciting and powerful approaches I have seen. I have selected them because they can serve as starting points for building a Peaceable Classroom curriculum, can be adapted to a variety of settings and ages, and can become powerful organizers for what happens in a classroom. In addition, many of the activities described here will also enhance the development of basic literacy and numeracy skills in young children, because they use basic academic skills to keep track of information and ideas in ways that are meaningful to young children.

9

Class Graphs: Building Community in Peaceable Classrooms

One way to promote peaceable living and learning is to collect meaningful information about the children in the class and represent it on simple graphs the children can understand. This approach can provide a wealth of developmentally appropriate curriculum activities that help achieve the goals of the Peaceable Classroom while incorporating much of the traditional curriculum of early childhood classrooms, such as foundations for literacy and numeracy.

One teacher used class graphs as a regular feature of her kindergarten Peaceable Classroom curriculum. She made a large blank graph on oak tag (approximately 2.5 feet by 4 feet) with four columns and ten rows, making squares the size of Polaroid photographs. She then laminated the whole sheet with clear plastic and stuck a piece of Velcro at the top of each square, so that the children's laminated photos (which had Velcro on their backs) could easily be placed on and off the graph.

When children visited the classroom before the start of the school year, the teacher took a Polaroid photograph of each child. Then, when they arrived on the first school day, she had the photo ready with each child's name on the bottom, a plastic laminated protective cover, and a piece of Velcro (or magnetic tape) on the back. The children indicated their responses to a question on the class graph by sticking their photos in the column with their choice written and symbolized at the bottom. Throughout the year, the children regularly gathered information about themselves and their diversity in this way and discussed it at class meetings.

Why Use Class Graphs?

- The graphs allow children to represent and compare in concrete, visible ways information about themselves—who they are as respected and safe individuals within a Peaceable Classroom community. Because of how they think, seeing information organized in this way can help children find meaning and make connections that would be hard to find and make on their own.

- The graphs regularly remind children of the importance and value of their diversity—who they are; what they think, feel, like, and do; and how they look.

- The graphs enhance children's mathematical skills by helping them see numerical information in pictorial form. Graphs make concepts such as "more than," "less than," or "the same as," "a lot" or "a little," "most" or "a few," "how many," "how many more," or "how many less" available to children in concrete and visible ways long before the children can understand them or use them to perform logical or symbolic operations.

- The graphs foster children's literacy skills. The sample class graphs described in this chapter provide a range of cues that help early readers and children who cannot read find ways to "read" the information on the graphs. For instance, by providing icons (simple pictorial representations that accompany each word, category, and number) and writing the children's names underneath their photos, the teacher helps children associate words and letters with meaningful information. In keeping with ideas about literacy development that grow out of the whole language or emergent literacy approach, as children learn to read class graphs, their actual literacy skills are enhanced.

Adapting Class Graphs to Different Ages and Abilities

- With preschool children, you may want to start with three-dimensional class graphs, where children actually use their bodies to represent where they go on the graph (for instance, ask children who like pizza to line up on one side and children who do not like pizza to line up on the other).

- Older children might get to the point where they can do their own surveys and graphs in the classroom on a variety of topics, which they share later with the class.

- You can ask children who have begun to list some mathematical conclusions about what they have "read" on the graph—for instance, "What is the most common way children get to school?"

Ideas for Infusing Class Graphs into the Curriculum

Here are several additional examples of how you can use class graphs with young children. The numbers of columns and rows in the graphs vary with the age of the children and the topic graphed.

Figure 9.1
OUR CLASS GRAPH

The Question
of the Day:

10 ⦿⦿⦿⦿⦿ ⦿⦿⦿⦿⦿	☐	☐	☐	☐
9 ⦿⦿⦿⦿⦿ ⦿⦿⦿⦿	☐	☐	☐	☐
8 ⦿⦿⦿⦿ ⦿⦿⦿⦿	☐	☐	☐	☐
7 ⦿⦿⦿ ⦿⦿⦿⦿	☐	☐	☐	☐
6 ⦿⦿⦿ ⦿⦿⦿	☐	☐	☐	☐
5 ⦿⦿ ⦿⦿⦿	☐	☐	☐	☐
4 ⦿⦿ ⦿⦿	☐	☐	☐	☐
3 ⦿⦿⦿	☐	☐	☐	☐
2 ⦿⦿	☐	☐	☐	☐
1 ⦿	☐	☐	☐	☐

☐ = Velcro

Class Graphs to Help in the Transition from Home to School

A kindergarten teacher used this graph on the first day of school as a way of greeting children when they arrived. (See Figure 9.2) She helped them find and choose the column where they wanted their photo, and then, at circle time, she had a brief discussion using the information on the graph to discuss the different ways children can feel on the first day of school, the things that make them feel that way, and how what happened during the day might affect how they feel at the present moment. This approach to starting school established right from the start that:

- the children's feelings and thoughts are important;
- diverse ideas are legitimate and valued;
- other children feel the same way they do (e.g., "I'm not the only one who is scared");
- the children are part of a community that cares about and takes care of its members.

The teacher returned to the graph at the end of the first week of school to discuss whether any of the children wanted to move their photo because their feelings had changed. Several children eagerly raised their hands.

Figure 9.2
OUR CLASS GRAPH

The Question of the Day:	Today I feel: ☺ ☹ 😨 ◯			
8 ・・・・ ・・・・	☐	☐	☐	☐
7 ・・・ ・・・・	☐	☐	☐	☐
6 ・・・ ・・・	☐	☐	☐	☐
5 ・・ ・・・	☐	☐	☐	☐
4 ・・ ・・	☐	☐	☐	☐
3 ・・・	☐	☐	☐	☐
2 ・・	☐	☐	☐	☐
1 ・	☐	☐	☐	☐
	Happy ☺	Sad ☹	Scared 😨	Other ◯

☐ = Velcro

Class Graphs to Develop Curriculum around a Personally Meaningful Theme

One teacher used this graph near the beginning of the year as part of a thematic curriculum unit titled "Getting to Know Us." She developed the unit to help the children with the transition from home to school, to help them feel comfortable with their classmates by discovering things they shared with each other, and to show them they were valued for who they were and what they thought. Each day, the teacher had the children do a graph on a different question about themselves, such as, "How did you get to school today?" (See Figure 9.3).

Because this teacher introduced graphs at the beginning of the year, the children quickly became comfortable using graphs as a central part of their daily circle time. Notice that the graph uses simple line drawings of vehicles to help children learn to complete and understand it independently.

Figure 9.3
OUR CLASS GRAPH

The Question of the Day: | How do you get to school?

	Car	Walk	Bus	Subway – T
8	☐	☐	☐	☐
7	☐	☐	☐	☐
6	☐	☐	☐	☐
5	☐	☐	☐	☐
4	☐	☐	☐	☐
3	☐	☐	☐	☐
2	☐	☐	☐	☐
1	☐	☐	☐	☐

This next graph was part of a first grade curriculum unit titled "Our Families." Focusing on numbers of people in the children's families provided an excellent way to discuss different kinds of families—an especially rich topic because the children in the class had many different family constellations (See Figure 9.4). But even classes without much obvious diversity will still find variations in family size.

Using this graph helped the children work out an understanding of what families are—in a way that promoted a sense of both the similarities and differences among their families. Children also brought in photographs of their families for use in conjunction with graph discussions. Among the math activities that developed from these discussions was one where the children took one Unifix cube (interlocking plastic blocks) for each family member and used the cubes to do calculations like: "What is the total number of people in all the families of the children in the class?" (It took an entire circle time discussion/problem-solving session to work this problem out.) The family puppets described in Chapter 11 provide another rich possibility for curriculum development for this unit.

Figure 9.4
OUR CLASS GRAPH

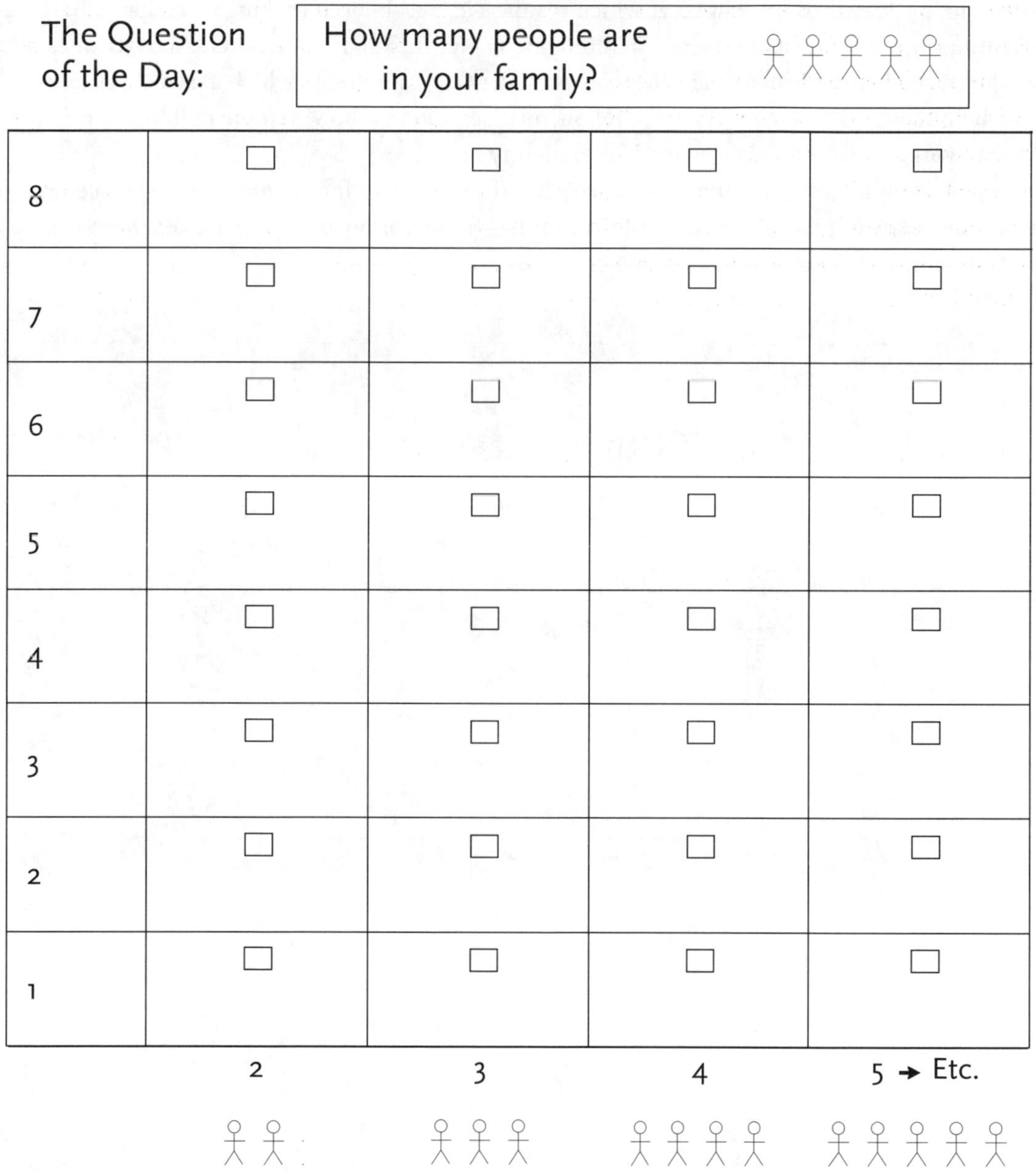

The Question
of the Day:

How many people are in your family?

8	☐	☐	☐	☐
7	☐	☐	☐	☐
6	☐	☐	☐	☐
5	☐	☐	☐	☐
4	☐	☐	☐	☐
3	☐	☐	☐	☐
2	☐	☐	☐	☐
1	☐	☐	☐	☐
	2	3	4	5 → Etc.

Class Graphs to Help Follow Up on Solutions to Class Problems

The graph in Figure 9.5 was developed as a follow-up activity to the discussion on "what to do when you need help" described in Chapter 4, which resulted in the children making a "Helper Chart" (See Figure 10.4) to encourage them to ask each other for help instead of the teacher. About a week after the children made the Helper Chart, the teacher made this class graph, which asked, "Did anyone ask you for help today?" It was the focus of a follow-up discussion on how well the children thought the chart was working and how they would like to modify it.

Graphs used in this way can provide a wonderful mechanism for ongoing group problem solving. And the simplicity of graphs with only two columns—for yes or no answers—makes them well suited for introducing class graphs to very young children.

Figure 9.5
OUR CLASS GRAPH

The Question of the Day:	Did anyone ask you for help today?	
8	☐	☐
7	☐	☐
6	☐	☐
5	☐	☐
4	☐	☐
3	☐	☐
2	☐	☐
1	☐	☐

YES Green   NO Red

☐ = Velcro

The next graph was used to help organize another follow-up discussion. The teacher wanted to check in with the children on how they thought the decision to have girls and boys team up in the block area was working as a solution to boys playing more than girls with the blocks (See the dialogue in Chapter 6). She started with simple yes or no questions on the graph. Was the solution leading to more girls going into the block area? Were children feeling more comfortable with each other when both boys and girls were there? Were there new things they should try?

Figure 9.6
OUR CLASS GRAPH

The Question of the Day:	Did you play in the blocks today?	
8	☐	☐
7	☐	☐
6	☐	☐
5	☐	☐
4	☐	☐
3	☐	☐
2	☐	☐
1	☐	☐

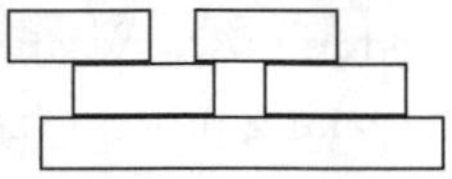

Class Graphs to Teach Democratic Decision Making

This classroom did a lot of cooking and baking. The children often helped plan menus for what they would prepare for class festivities. Here is a two-column graph (See Figure 9.7) the teacher used to take a vote on whether the children wanted to bake cookies or muffins for José's class birthday party.

Class Graphs used in this way can provide a developmentally appropriate format for introducing a democratic decision making process (i.e., voting) to young children. It is not so much the idea of voting that is focused on, as the process of participating in collective decision-making. In order to build an understanding of a shared decision-making process, young children need many concrete and meaningful opportunities to see how their desires and ideas (i.e., votes) contribute to what actually happens in the classroom. Do not be too surprised if the voting results are at first treated differently by the children than how you intended to use them. Young children are often more bound by what they want and whether they get it than by what the numbers in the vote say. And, trying to reach a decision everyone can accept to some degree still needs to be a central goal even when you introduce voting.

Two-column graphs like this one, where there are only two choices to be made (often either "yes" or "no"), can be an effective way to introduce class graphs to very young children who have a hard time thinking about more than one thing at a time. Even when the children are not fully functioning counters, they can see which of the two columns of photos is the highest.

Figure 9.7
OUR CLASS GRAPH

The Question
of the Day:

What should we bake for Jose's Birthday?

10 • • • • • • • • • •	☐	☐
9 • • • • • • • • •	☐	☐
8 • • • • • • • •	☐	☐
7 • • • • • • •	☐	☐
6 • • • • • •	☐	☐
5 • • • • •	☐	☐
4 • • • •	☐	☐
3 • • •	☐	☐
2 • •	☐	☐
1 •	☐	☐
	 oatmeal cookies	 corn muffins

Class Charts:
Building Predictable Rituals,
Routines, and a Sense of Safety

Young children need help actively learning how cooperative communities work and how to be responsible, contributing members of these communities. This process can be helped immeasurably by establishing predictable and understandable rules, rituals, and routines to guide children's actions in concrete ways. I have seen many teachers use class charts to develop such structures in their Peaceable Classrooms.

Using Class Charts to Help Children Function as Autonomous Learners and Responsible Community Members

At the beginning of the year, class charts prepared in advance by teachers can help children learn simple things about how to function in their classroom. The "Class Cleanup Jobs" (Figure 10.1), "Choice Board" (Figure 10.2), and "Our Daily Schedule" charts (Figure 10.3) are examples of the kind of charts teachers can use from the start of the school year to help children learn to function as autonomous and responsible members of their Peaceable Classrooms. Simple versions of these charts—with names and photos or pictures—can work effectively for children as young as three.

The teachers who made these charts did not expect the children to be able to use them fully at the start. For instance, knowing it is their job to clean up the blocks only has meaning for children when they know exactly what they need to do to clean up the blocks. Choosing the art area on the Choice Board only has meaning when you know how to use the art materials constructively.

Therefore, helping children learn to use class charts is a vital part of your Peaceable Classroom curriculum during the first weeks of school. I have seen teachers do this in ways that also incorporate the curriculum they are "supposed" to be covering—for instance, reading and math. Each of these beginning-of-the-year charts evolved and changed as the year progressed, based on the issues the children raised once they became fully comfortable with how the charts worked.

Class Cleanup Chart

There are many ways to structure the cleanup of a classroom. One way, which can effectively promote a sense of shared responsibility and community in young children, is to use a Class Cleanup Chart. (Figure 10.1) This chart consists of two concentric cardboard circles held together at the center by a brass paper fastener. Pairs of children are assigned jobs for a week. Each Monday, the inner circle is moved clockwise by one child's name; so that one child in a pair stays with the same job for the next week with a new partner, and the other child moves on to the next job. This system works extremely well at the beginning of the year, because once one child knows a job, a continuous process of teaching it to the next child begins, until all the children have learned all the jobs.

Figure 10.1
CLASS CLEANUP JOBS

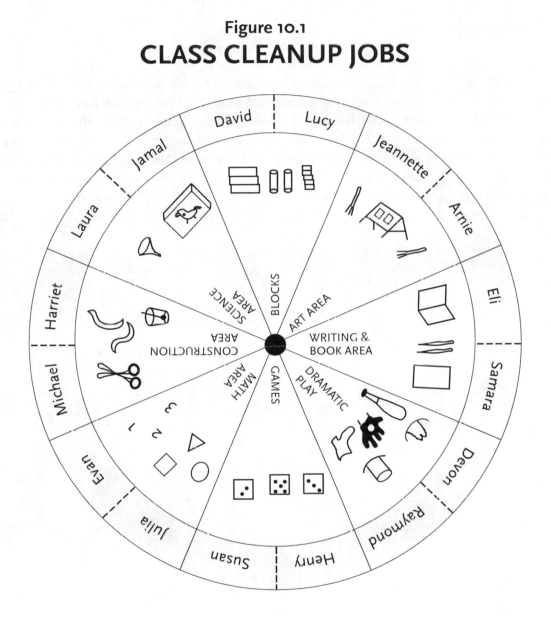

Choice Board

The Choice Board (Figure 10.2) is kept in the class meeting area so that children can make choices at the end of the early morning meeting, when the day's activities and plans are discussed. The little squares on the right are self-adhesive Velcro pieces onto which children can place their personal name circles which are stored at the bottom of the board on Velcro fasteners. The number of Velcro squares next to each activity indicates the number of children who can choose that area. The rectangle activity cards on the left, with the activities listed by word and symbol, are also attached to the board with Velcro, so that they can be put on and taken off of the board, depending on what activity areas are open on a given day. Usually an activity card stays up for at least a week, so that all the children trust that they will get a turn, even with very popular activities, and children who get involved with an activity know they will be able to choose it again to continue their work.

Figure 10.2

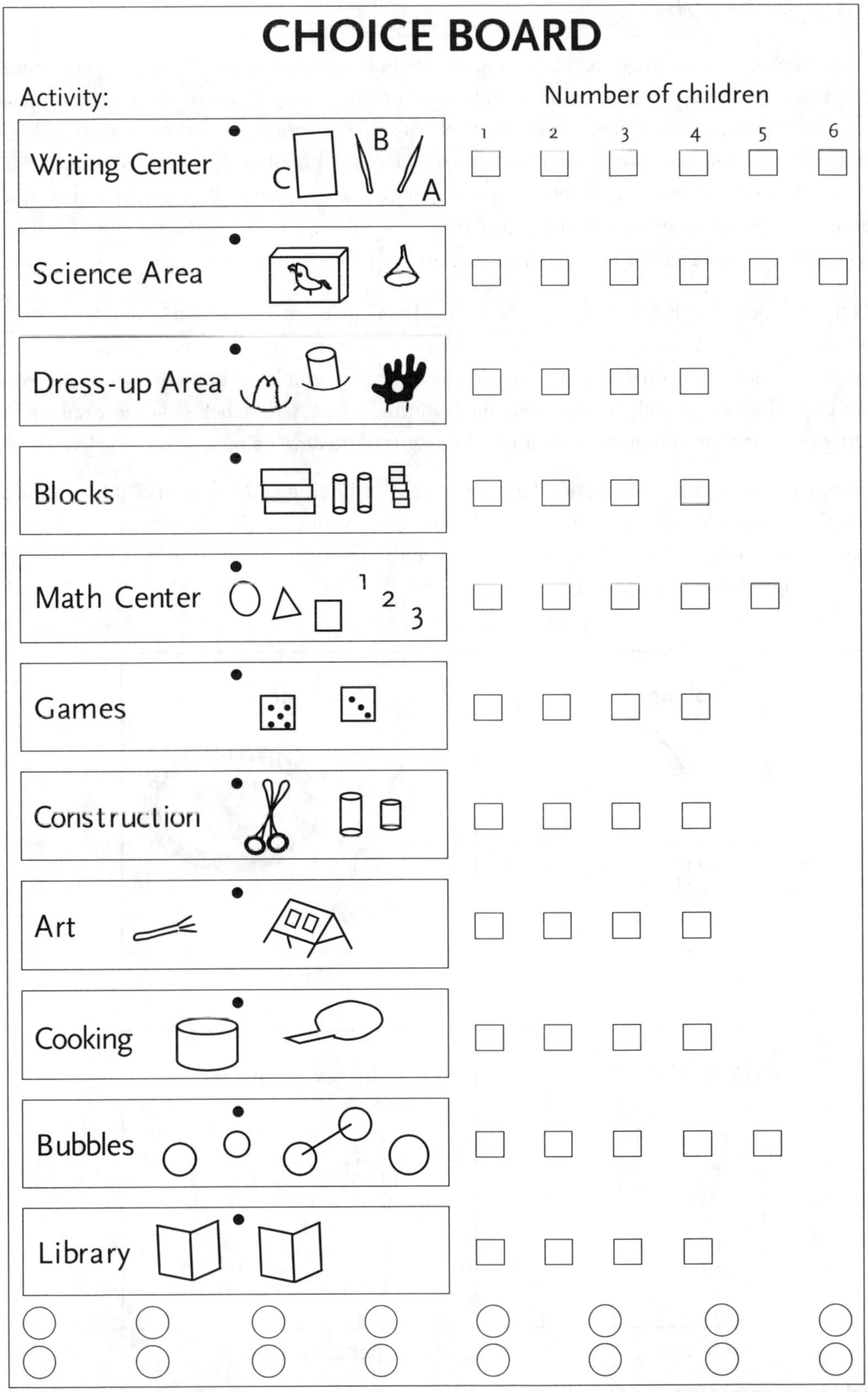

CHOICE BOARD

Activity: Number of children

= velcro fasteners
(note: the number of fasteners indicates how many children can go to that area)
= name labels storage area

Our Daily Schedule

The Our Daily Schedule (Figure 10.3) chart represents in words and pictures the fixed sequence of daily activities in a classroom. The column on the right contains information about specific activities that will occur on a given day. The teacher uses self-adhesive magnetic tape (Velcro would also work) to attach cards with special activities to the chart each day: what book will be read at class meeting, what fruit will be served at snack, whether a particular child's birthday will be celebrated at lunch, or what theme will be set up in the dramatic play area.

This daily schedule chart serves two vital functions:

- When the children arrive, it provides a focus for a brief circle time discussion about the day. The class refers back to it throughout the day as needed, so that the children can learn the rhythm and sequence of their day, know what special activities to expect, and learn to predict when they will be picked up. This is especially reassuring at the beginning of the year, when children need a lot of help finding predictability and order in their day, prerequisites to developing a sense of safety and trust.

- It greatly improved communication between school and home and between children and parents about the children's daily lives at school. The chart was kept near the classroom entrance at the beginning and end of the school day, so that parents could check it and discuss it with their children at drop-off and pickup times.

Sample activity cards to go on "Our Daily Schedule" using velcro.

Figure 10.3

OUR DAILY SCHEDULE

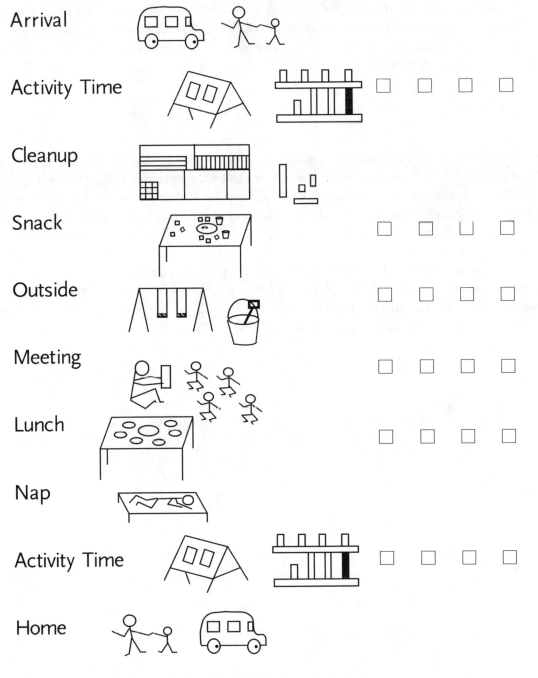

☐ = self adhesive magnetic tape (onto which activity cards
  with magnetic tape on back can be stuck)

Using Class Charts to Aid Group Problem Solving and Community Building

Class charts can help build a feeling of community, as well as group problem-solving abilities. Brainstorming solutions to a problem can help children try out new, positive ways of participating in the classroom. By referring back to the charts regularly to build on or modify their solutions based on direct experience, children become involved in the dynamic process of forging their own unique Peaceable Classroom community.

Helper Chart

This Helper Chart (Figure 10.4) grew out of the dialogue about getting help in the classroom when the teacher is busy, as described in Chapter 4, "Building a Peaceable Classroom through Give-and-Take Dialogues." The categories and names on the chart were developed by the children.

The teacher displayed the Helper Chart prominently, so that children could easily remember to use it as needed. After about a week, she used the "Did Anyone Ask You for Help Today?" class graph (Figure 9.5) as the basis for a discussion with the children about how the chart was working and how they might like to change it.

This sequence of activities—1) having a dialogue about a class problem, 2) developing and trying out a solution using a class chart, and 3) using a class graph to discuss how well the solution was working after the children had tried it out—shows how teachers can build a wide range of curriculum activities around Peaceable Classroom goals and issues.

Figure 10.4

HELPER CHART
(Who to ask for help)

- Counting things
  Raymond
  Elisha

- Building with blocks
  Jackson

- Washing tables
  Jenna
  Nathania

- Writing letters in your name
  Sara
  Sam
  Henry

- Using scissors and glue
  Sam
  Darrah
  Sally

- Swinging on a swing
  Danielle
  Henry

- Hanging up wet paintings
  Tosca
  Raymond

- Zipping and buttoning (but not tying)
  Jackson
  Sally

- Playing hospital
  Sara
  Jason

- Washing paintbrushes
  Kendra
  Nathania

- Running
  Kevin
  Kendra

- Feeding the gerbil
  Harold
  Raymond

- Making things with playdough
  Dore
  Jenna
  Harold

- Drawing Ninja Turtles
  Evan
  Jason

Using a Class Chart to Create a Class History

Young children only gradually come to realize that history consists of a logical sequence of events connected to the present. They tend to think about time in the here and now, where the past is what happened "before now," and the future is what will happen "after now." Yet, to understand how Peaceable Communities work and how they can change in the future, one must first understand how they came to be the way they are now—their history. One powerful, developmentally appropriate way to help children build an understanding of history and time is to "build history" with them, using their shared, concrete experiences in their Peaceable Classroom.

To do this, one kindergarten teacher used an ongoing Class History Chart (Figure 10.5). The children counted the number of days they had been at school and built a number line, adding one number each day. Meanwhile, the teacher recorded one special event or activity for each day on a three-inch by six-inch file card, on which she wrote a few words and drew a simple picture the children could "read." At a daily meeting time, when the children added the number of the day to their number line, they also "read" the "event of the day" card and placed it up with that day's number. Gradually, the special events number line stretched all around the classroom and served as a history of the class' year to which the children could easily refer. On their hundredth day in school, the children had a special celebration, reviewed their class history chart, and reminisced about their accomplishments and how different things felt now from the way they did at the beginning of the number line.

Building a Class History Chart in this way helps young children:

- learn about history and time in concrete terms they can understand;

- learn about numbers in a meaningful context—for instance, how to read and record them and how they are sequenced and grow;

- learn literacy skills as they "read" each day's symbol that is tied to a meaningful experience and then, gradually, figure out the words associated with those symbols;

- experience directly that they are participating members of a caring, cooperative community that has built a shared history together.

One teacher used a variation of this Class History Chart with three-year-olds. She made a pictorial class history in an album that circulated to homes, helping create a sense of community among the children, home, and school, and giving parents something concrete to talk about with their children. Some teachers who use class history charts with older children plan "one hundredth day in school" celebrations which include both special acknowledgements of what the classroom community has accomplished in 100 days together as well as activities focusing on the number 100.

Figure 10.5

CLASS HISTORY CHART

1	2	3	4	5
Today is our 1st day together. 	Today is our 1st day of the Library. 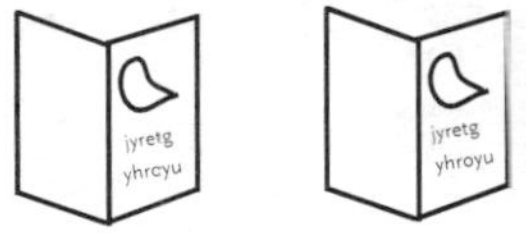	Today is Joanna's Birthday. 	Today we baked Pizza. 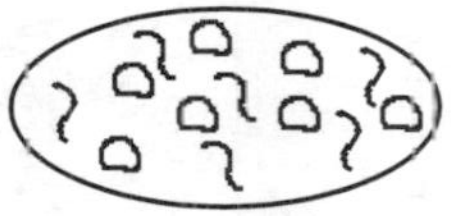	Today is the end of our 1st week of school. 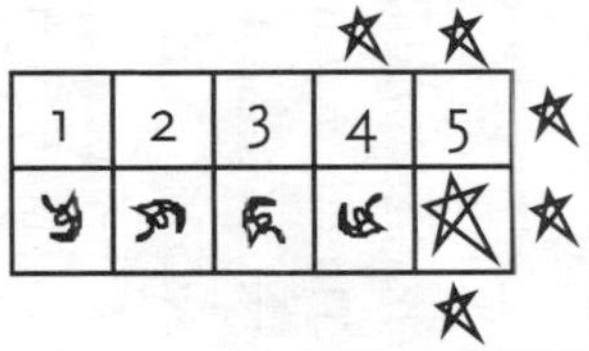

50	51	52	53	54
Today we counted our pockets. We had 47 pockets. 	Today we finished reading "Elmer's Dragon". 	Today we ate the pumpkin pie we made. (It was good.) 	Today Nanda came back to school with a cast on her leg. 	Today Henry's dad came to teach us how to make casts for our fingers. 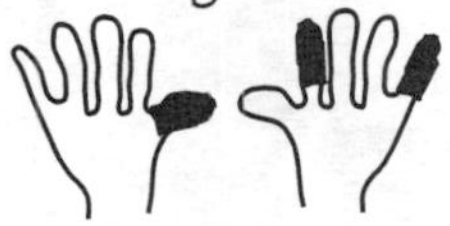

Ways to Be Powerful in the Blue Room

This chart (Figure 10.6) was developed by the children in a first and second grade classroom. They redefined what it meant to be powerful. They had been having difficulty resolving conflicts, such as who got to play with whom and who used which materials. They were also having problems with teasing and put-downs. To solve these problems, children came up with the items on the chart and discussed ways to put each into practice. They agreed to watch for examples of classmates behaving in these "powerful" ways and were regularly given opportunities to share their observations at class meetings.

This group validation of their positive behavior helped the children experience the positive effects of their own (and others') power and built a sense of community and shared responsibility. It provided them a wonderful opportunity to have "power with" rather than "power over" others. In the process of developing and using the chart, classroom and playground behavior improved dramatically.

Figure 10.6
WAYS TO BE POWERFUL
IN THE BLUE ROOM

YOU ARE POWERFUL WHEN YOU:

- help each other
- make a new friend
- say you're sorry
- try to get along with each other
- stop a fight
- walk away or ignore someone who is bothering you
- use words (not fists) when you're upset
- share blocks, markers, toys, games
- get help on work or help someone doing work
- do good work
- invite people to play with you
- ask if you can join a group
- help someone who is hurt or sad

11

Class Games: Promoting Cooperation, Perspective-Taking, and a Sense of Community

Learning to help each other and work together on shared goals is central to living in a Peaceable Classroom. Yet, because of their static thinking, egocentrism, and tendency to think about only one thing at a time, it can be a big challenge for young children to engage successfully with others in give-and-take, cooperative interactions. In the early years, games that loosely structure interactions around a skill or goal help young children learn to engage in give-and-take activities with others. These games can also help counteract the lessons many young children learn when they are exposed too early to competitive games. And the games lend themselves to a holistic curriculum where the content of the games often can relate to a specific subject area, concept, or skill.[1]

Class games for young children will not always look like what people commonly call games. Young children are only beginning to learn how to use formal rules to guide their behavior with others. They may realize that rules are used to regulate their own behavior, but they often do not focus on the need for everyone playing a game to follow the same rules or the importance of playing by the same rules throughout the game. Often, even when children can state a rule, translating their words into consistent actions can be a difficult next step.

Therefore, it is a challenge to develop class games for young children that not only match their abilities and interests, but also promote cooperation and fun rather than competition and misery. You will need to put aside your adult ideas about games and rules, as well as concepts like winning, losing, competing, and cheating. Pushing children into following rules they cannot yet understand can easily lead to rigid, competitive, and stressful participation in games, which does nothing to promote the goals of a Peaceable Classroom.

On the other hand, when children do succeed at helping one another accomplish a goal, their ability to participate in a Peaceable Classroom expands and strengthens. Working

---

[1] For a wealth of additional ideas for cooperative games and peacemaking activities that can be incorporated into your Peaceable Classroom see: *Early Childhood Adventures in Peacemaking (2nd Edition)* by W. J. Kreidler and S. Whittall (Cambridge, MA: Educators for Social Responsibility, 1999). For a more complete discussion of how young children learn to understand and use rules, see *Group Games in Early Education* by C. Kamii and R. DeVries (Washington, DC: National Association for the Education of Young Children, 1980).

together can help them learn to take each other's points of view into account when deciding how to act. Moreover, it can give them the satisfaction of contributing and accomplishing something tangible through working with other children.

Class games for young children rarely have highly structured or complicated rules. Sometimes, when you help the children elaborate a give-and-take activity or game they began on their own, the rules originate from the children themselves. At other times, you can give them a starting point for a class game and then help the children adapt and mold it as they play.

However when a class game starts, it is often most exciting and valuable when you follow the children's lead as their play progresses and help the game develop into a regular and familiar classroom ritual. As you do this, you'll have many opportunities for periodic give-and-take discussions about such things as:

- what has happened with the game so far;

- the children's ideas about how to continue to expand on and vary the game;

- problems that have arisen and the children's ideas about how to solve them.

Pair Paintings: Class Games Started by Children

One teacher of four-year-olds reorganized her painting area when she saw two boys create a give-and-take game for painting shared pictures at the easel. The boys were taking turns brushing paint strokes onto a large piece of paper, adding onto each other's lines. Each time one added a stroke, he chanted, "Now this goes on yours." They repeated this process over and over, back and forth. As they continued painting, they speeded up their strokes and chants, and several other children came to watch. The teacher and observers began to chant with the painters.

When the two boys finished their cooperative painting, the teacher quickly made more room around the easel, so that other pairs of children could work at it together. All morning, pairs of children used the boys' approach to paintings. Over the next several days, the easel was constantly in use by children developing variations on the pair painting game, including:

- chants and actions that focused on

  - color ("Now I'm putting black on yours." "Now I'm putting blue on yours."),

  - specific kinds of brush strokes ("Now here goes a dot." "Now here goes a circle.");

- back-and-forth chants sung to familiar tunes;

- efforts to represent real objects ("Now here goes an eye on the face." "Now here goes a mouth on the face.");

- paintings and chants where three or more children participated.

The teacher regularly asked children to share at class meetings how they had made their pair paintings. With her help, they showed the paintings, described how they had worked together, and recited the chants they used. Thus, not only were these children gaining experience with give-and-take actions when they painted, the teacher was also helping them see that their efforts to work together toward unique ideas were valued. At the same time, by sharing their painting techniques, they were giving each other new ideas to try when they did their next pair paintings at the easel.

Gradually, the idea of working together in pairs spread to other areas of the classroom.

- Some children tried paired block building, where children took turns adding blocks to a building.

- Several used the give-and-take approach at cleanup time, alternating putting objects like blocks back on the shelf.

- Each time the children came up with a new use of the pair game the teacher would ask them to tell about it at a class meeting.

Thus, while the teacher could never have predicted where the pair paintings would lead, it became a central theme or ritual for organizing the social interactions and curriculum in that Peaceable Classroom. As the children played their pair games, they were also developing language and representational skills, as well as such concepts as logical causality, reciprocity, and color mixing.

Beanbag Games: Class Games Started by the Teacher

One kindergarten teacher used beanbags to introduce a teacher-guided class game to her children. She made enough beanbags (approximately three inches by three inches) for every child in her class. First, at class meeting she gave each child a beanbag to try to balance on his or her head. Sitting and balancing was not too hard for the children, but walking around posed a major challenge. Several children became frustrated over how often their beanbags fell, so the children had a brief discussion and decided to help each other learn to balance the beanbags.

The next day, the teacher grouped the children in pairs. One child balanced the beanbag, while the other coached the first child about how to walk and returned the beanbag to the "balancer's" head when it fell. Then the children switched roles. The give-and-take of children coaching each other required that the coach learn to de-center and pay attention to the actions and needs of the balancer. Each child had an opportunity to experience both needing and giving help. The children also saw the impressive progress they made learning to balance the beanbags.

The children asked to play this class game regularly and seemed to enjoy their growing mastery of balancing beanbags on their heads. Several variations of the "beanbag helper game" later evolved, including:

- trying to move at varying speeds—from slow motion to fast;

- using a variety of motions while the beanbag is on a child's head—hopping on two feet and one foot, standing on one foot and on tiptoes, and trying to move from standing to sitting and vice versa;

- trying to balance the beanbags on other parts of the body, such as shoulders, knees, and feet;

- first counting and then using a timer to see how long one could keep the beanbag on one's head;

- trying to balance other things on children's heads, such as mittens (a good item to start with for children younger than five), small blocks, and stuffed animals.

Because of the children's continuing interest in beanbag games, the teacher eventually introduced the "frozen beanbag game." Though still grouped in pairs, all the children had their own beanbags with both children in a pair trying to balance their beanbags at once. When a beanbag fell off one child's head, that child had to freeze until the other child bent down (without dropping his or her own beanbag!) and returned the fallen beanbag to its rightful place. If, as often happened, both children in a pair dropped their beanbags, they both froze. The game continued until everyone was frozen (which did not take very long when the game was first introduced). Later, the class decided that two children would be specially designated as "defrosters." It was their job to return the beanbags to frozen partners' heads, thereby keeping the game going indefinitely.

The children's idea of adding the defroster role to their game illustrates clearly how class games can encourage children to find better ways to help each other succeed. This contrasts with so many of the games children play outside of Peaceable Classrooms that involve finding better ways to compete with each other.

The frozen beanbag game added an exciting new give-and-take interaction to the children's repertoire. It also created a special challenge by requiring each child to think about at least two things at once: "What is happening to my beanbag and my partner's beanbag?" and "What do I need to do to keep my beanbag balanced on my head while I bend down to get my partner's beanbag and put it back on my partner's head?" As they worked on questions like these, the children were also experimenting with such scientific concepts as cause and effect, gravity, and balance.

Guidelines for Practice: Using Group Games with Children

- Watch the children to get ideas for activities you can help them develop into class games.

- At class meeting or small-group times, introduce new group games that can evolve as the children play.

- Consult curriculum and activity guidebooks to get ideas for starting points for new games, but you will often want to adapt to meet the needs and goals of your Peaceable Classroom.

- Do not worry about the children following the "rules" of a game too closely; rather, help them adapt and change the rules as they play.

- Develop games that promote cooperation, collaboration, and fun rather than competition, winning and losing, and wounded feelings.

- Follow the children's lead as their play progresses to help them further develop their games.

- Use the children's suggestions for changing a game as occasions for shared decision making.

- When children have a problem succeeding at a game, take advantage of the chance to support their efforts to learn how to help each other succeed.

- Make a few class games into regular classroom rituals; this can help the children develop a sense of predictability, shared experience, and community.

Creating Your Own Class Games

Pair paintings and paired beanbag games are two examples of teachers helping children turn small classroom events into long-term and meaningful learning activities. Rarely will it matter what the specific games are; what really matters is the give-and-take interactions that evolve.

Once you begin looking for starting points for class games, you are likely to find that the possibilities are endless. The children will usually be your greatest resource. Many curriculum guides and manuals also provide ideas for games and activities that you can adapt to support the aims of class games described here (See *Resources*).

Class Puppets: Promoting Problem Solving, Conflict Resolution, and Cooperative Learning

Puppets provide another concrete and visible way to teach young children vital skills for actively participating in a Peaceable Classroom.[1] You can use them to work on many of the same issues and content you might discuss using give-and-take dialogues.

Using "Us" Puppets to Act Out Experience

Simple puppets of each child in your class (and yourself and other adults, too) can be used to dramatize stories about themselves, their classmates, and their shared class experiences. One teacher made "Us" puppets by taking a full-body photograph of each child, cutting out the child's form, and mounting it on a tongue depressor. Another teacher put photos of all the children on a block of wood the size of a unit block; these "us blocks" were also used by children in their regular block and other minature world play to act out dramas involving themselves. Children can also make little self-portraits to glue to sticks (it may be hard to recognize the self-portraits of young children, but that's okay). Using puppets, young children can gradually learn to act out and work on simple scenarios from their experience. They can use the puppets to:

- **Recreate positive class experiences with each other.** Children can use their "Us" puppets to act out something they enjoyed doing together in the classroom. Even young children will enjoy having their own puppet sing favorite songs, "read" familiar books, or pretend to eat a meal. Older children will want to act out more detailed scenarios interacting with other children's puppets— for instance, dramatizing a recent in-class birthday party or field trip.

- **Act out successful problem-solving and conflict resolution situations.** When children successfully work out a problem or conflict, they can recount the experience with puppets as a way to help their classmates learn more about problem-solving and as a means of sharing their successes with others. With young children, it often works best to tell the story yourself as the children move their puppets to act out the story (to the extent that they are able). Gradually, they can begin to fill in pieces of the story on their own and with your help build up to telling the whole story themselves.

---

[1] "Class puppets" have been adapted for younger children from "problem puppets" which were developed by William Kreidler for elementary school age children. Problem puppets are described in *Creative Conflict Resolution: More Than 200 Activities for Keeping Peace in the Classroom* (Scott Foresman & Co., Glencoe IL, 1984). For resources on using puppets and dolls to work especially on anti-bias issues with young children see the description of "Persona Dolls" in *The Anti-bias Curriculum* by L. Derman-Sparks et al. (Washington, DC: National Association for the Education of Young Children, 1989) and *Kids Like Us: Using Persona Dolls in the Classroom* by T. Whitney (St. Paul, MN: Redleaf Press, 1999).

- **Reenact conflicts and interpersonal problems and try out proposed solutions.** Puppets can be used to act out both conflicts the children have actually had and pretend conflicts from books or made up by you to work on a particular issue. At first, you will need to help the children use the puppets to reenact conflicts and problems, filling in crucial information and engaging the children in give-and-take dialogue about the conflict. For instance, after a puppet says something, you can turn to the children to see if they agree, or ask them what the puppet might have said or done instead. You can also ask the children for ideas to help a puppet solve a problem and then have the puppet react to their ideas.

"Us" Puppets Promote the Goals of Peaceable Classrooms

When used to work on these kinds of in-class experiences, "Us" puppets provide young children with a meaningful and safe way of learning to live and work together in a Peaceable Classroom. They help children:

- reenact a wide range of concrete experiences with others, both positive and negative, in order to deepen their understanding, skill, and sense of control and mastery;

- feel they belong to a community that cares about how people treat one another and values working together on conflicts and problems;

- reenact their conflicts or problems once they have calmed down, so they can develop new ways of understanding and problem solving;

- try out one or more solutions to a conflict or problem, get a sense of how that solution feels, and then decide whether they really want to try it out;

- talk about a difficult situation with others in a concrete and direct way that avoids the high stakes and emotions of real-world interactions;

- experience control and mastery as they distance themselves from real-life situations that may have felt threatening when they happened;

- develop confidence and skill with the whole process of trying out ideas, taking risks, and listening to others;

- get vicarious satisfaction and emotional release by expressing ideas, feelings, and behaviors that might not be acceptable in real life—for instance, aggression, anger, silliness.

"Us" Puppets Match Children's Developmental Level

"Us" puppets also can help young children expand and complicate their thinking, and further develop cognitive skills for solving problems peacefully and working together cooperatively. For instance, by working with puppets, children can be helped to:

- move from static thinking about experiences to more dynamic thinking, as they use the puppets to transform and vary a given event over and over;

- move from seeing one aspect of a situation at a time to seeing many aspects and from seeing isolated parts of a situation to seeing a more integrated whole, as they use puppets to organize events into a logical sequence and make causal connections between them;

- shift from seeing only one point of view (usually their own) to seeing more than one viewpoint and even how two viewpoints interact with one another, as they see their various roles and perspectives played out in a nonthreatening situation.

Additional Ideas for Using Class Puppets in Peaceable Classrooms

Once children become comfortable using "Us" puppets, there are many other meaningful ways to incorporate puppets into your Peaceable Classroom.

- **Puppets of favorite book characters.** Using the tongue depressor technique described above, you can make puppets of the characters in your children's favorite stories. Children can then act out parts or all of a story. Younger children will probably just enjoy imitating simple actions and sounds of one character puppet at a time.

- **Puppets of children's favorite media characters.** Puppets of favorite TV and movie characters can help children actively transform what they have seen in the media into something meaningful to them. In addition, children can use puppets to transcend the content they receive from TV, moving the characters away from the usual violence, stereotyping, and predictably simplistic plots. Such puppets can help children get beyond the imitative play that often results from using the highly realistic toys that accompany TV shows.

    Using media puppets can also provide insight into what meanings children are making from the shows they watch. With this information, you can begin to develop curriculum activities and give-and-take dialogues that help to modify the meanings children have made.

    One teacher of four- and five-year-olds made puppets of the Teenage Mutant Ninja Turtles with the children and used them to work on the narrow content from the Turtles that children were bringing to the classroom. Another teacher of first-graders made Wizard of Oz puppets with her children and used them to recreate the children's favorite parts of the movie.

- **Puppets of the children's families.** Children can also make simple puppets of family members and use them to reenact important experiences at home. Small photos of family members glued to tongue depressors work wonderfully, especially with younger children, but simple drawings can also work well.

    Family puppets can be especially valuable for children when some milestone occurs in the family. For instance, when a new sibling is born, the child can use puppets to work on feelings about the new baby and figure out positive ways he or she might interact with the baby. Family puppets can also help build home-school connections for children and can supplement curriculum on diversity among the children's families.

Guidelines for Using Class Puppets with Children

- **Children need a lot of help from you in learning how to use puppets productively and nonviolently.** Often, the first thing a child does with a puppet—especially if it fits over the hand—is to punch others with it. Be prepared to teach appealing alternative behaviors.

- **Start simply and use the puppets yourself at first, modeling the kinds of things children can do with them.**

- **Provide or make the first puppets yourself.** Children need to know something about what a puppet is and what it can do before they are ready to make one themselves.

- **Start with simple, small puppets that are less likely to suggest fighting or aggression (as puppets that cover the hand often do).** For instance, as suggested above, use small cutout cardboard figures glued to wooden tongue depressors or craft sticks. Later, old socks with buttons sewn on for eyes can also make simple, appealing, and open-ended puppets.

- **Start by working on issues that are not highly emotional or volatile.** In this way, children can develop skills for using puppets before they bring strong emotions into the act.

- **In their work with the puppets, encourage the children to tap into the wide range of skills they are learning from their give-and-take dialogues.** For instance, try getting the puppets to use words children have learned, brainstorm solutions to problems, or engage in give-and-take interactions with other puppets.

- **Bring in a wide range of issues that show children the rich possibilities of class puppets.**

- **Gradually increase children's opportunities to use familiar puppets without your help—individually and in small groups.** For instance, leave the puppets in a designated area in the classroom where children are free to play with them in an open-ended way, or work on a problem that has come up for them.

Class Conflict Stories: Promoting Group Problem Solving and Literacy

A central component of many early literacy programs is having children write their own books. Through bookmaking, children use their own words and drawings to tell personally meaningful stories. As they do, they are learning key aspects of the literacy process—how to make letters and sounds fit together to create words and create meaning, how to sequence events in a logical way, how to transform concrete experience into written words and pictures, and how to get meaningful information from words and pictures as they reread what they wrote.

Class Conflict Stories are books the teacher and children make together that are based on problems and conflicts that have come up in the classroom. Writing Class Conflict Stories can support the same literacy goals of children's bookmaking as well as your efforts to teach children how to resolve their conflicts peaceably. Like Problem Puppets (see Chapter 12), they furnish children with an opportunity to work together, using the approach to conflict resolution described throughout this book, to develop strategies for solving problems and conflicts they have with each other. They provide a technique for working out resolutions to real life conflicts removed from the immediacy of the conflict situation. They also help children become invested in trying out the ideas they come up with for the stories in their classroom community.

Here is a teacher's account of how she creates Class Conflict Stories with preschoolers and kindergarteners as part of her overall Peaceable Classroom curriculum:[1]

> I introduce class meetings early in the year and use them as an opportunity to raise issues that I've noticed have come up with the children. As the children become familiar with the meeting process, they begin to bring in their own issues to put on the agenda as well.
>
> Then, I open the meeting with the issue by stating what I have seen, such as, 'I have noticed many kids playing chase lately. Does anyone have anything they want to share about the game?' Or, as a follow-up to an early discussion about issues at snack, I might ask, 'How are things going with snack lately?' I open it with as little bias as possible so that the children feel comfortable sharing any thoughts about the subject.

[1]Special thanks to Sarae Pacetta, Wheelock College graduate student, for sharing this approach to "Class Conflict Stories" which she developed in her classroom, as well as the actual story that she created with the children which illustrates this chapter.

Children also gradually learn to raise their own issues in terms of seeking help to solve a problem, such as, 'We have been running out of juice lately, and I am wondering why and what we can do.'

There are several ways I facilitate the discussion during the meeting. I tend to ask lots of questions to help children explain and develop their ideas and move the discussion along. I ask children to rephrase what has been said when there is confusion. I make sure all voices are listened to and respected. Once we are clear on the issues, I guide the class toward making a plan on how to solve the problem by helping children share their ideas about how it might be solved.

Sometimes we make Class Conflict Story books from the topics of our class meetings. Other times we write our stories using pretend situations I make up that are based on problems I've noticed but want to address in a less personal way. We usually use a 'choose your own adventure' format, where the problem is stated (and drawn) in the first pages (often by me). Then children write and illustrate their ideas for various possible endings to the problem. Sometimes, we use a format in which each child proposes a solution to a problem and illustrates his or her page. Other times we brainstorm as a group and work on the pages with partners. When the children are done I assemble the pages into a book.

This process helps children build skills in creative thinking and problem solving, and expand their abilities to listen to others and try out others' ideas. For my preschoolers and kindergartners, having their ideas in print is powerful. So is seeing the connection between the printed page and their actions solving problems.

The books are always class favorites when we put them in the class library and they are 'read' constantly. They have become an important part of our class culture, and kids refer to them frequently in play and in conflicts.

Guidelines for Practice: Beginning to Create Class Conflict Stories

- **Decide on the conflict or problem you want the children to talk and "write" about.** It may be one you have noticed yourself, or one that children have raised with you. When first introducing the idea of conflict stories to the children try to choose a conflict that is not very emotionally loaded for the children and which is unlikely to involve very complicated negotiations.

- **As illustrated in the two Class Conflict Stories here, make simple drawings (with words) in advance of the class meeting that lay out the salient aspects of the problem for the children.**

- **Have a meeting where you share the problem you have prepared with the children.** As with the approach to conflict resolution described throughout this book, get the children's ideas about the problem and then share their individual ideas about what should happen to solve the problem.

- **Children then create their own page for the book that illustrates their solutions.** They either "write" or dictate to you the text that goes with their pictures.

- **Assemble your and the children's work into a book (laminated if possible).**

Figure 13.1
SAMPLE CONFLICT STORY

IT WAS LUNCH TIME, AND JESS AND MATTEO WERE SITTING DOWN AT THE TABLE. "I HAVE PIZZA!" SAID MATTEO. "I HAVE TOFU!" SAID JESS. ①

BILL CAME UP TO THE TABLE TO SIT DOWN. "YOU CAN'T SIT HERE. I'M SAVING THE SPOT FOR NEERA." SAID JESS. "ANYWAY," SAID MATTEO, "YOU HAVE A FUNNY LOOKING LUNCH BOX." ②

BILL LOOKED AT HIS LUNCH BOX. IT WAS HIS FAVORITE COLOR - GREEN - AND HE DIDN'T SEE WHAT WAS SO FUNNY ABOUT IT. ③

"FUNNY LUNCH BOX! FUNNY LUNCH BOX!" CHANTED JESS AND MATTEO. BILL WENT OVER TO THE OTHER TABLE AND SAT DOWN, FEELING HURT AND LEFT OUT. ④

BILL'S FRIEND JULIET HAD HEARD WHAT HAPPENED TO BILL AND COULD TELL HE WAS FEELING BADLY. WHAT COULD SHE DO? ⑤

An example of a class conflict story, "What Can You Do?", created by Sarae Pacetta and her preschool class. It is a fictional version of a problem the children were having at the time. Here are the pages Sarae made to introduce the problem to the children.

Figure 13.1, *continued*

Here are examples of solutions the children came up with for their conflict story.

- **At the next class meeting, read the story and talk about the various solutions and how children think they might work.** Choose which one/s to try.

- **Place the book in your classroom library** so children can select it to "read" and discuss again in the future.

Additional Ideas for Using Class Conflict Stories in Peaceable Classrooms

- Return to previously completed conflict stories regularly with the children by reading and discussing them at class meetings. This helps children review what they have already learned about resolving conflicts and add new ideas about what could happen based on experiences they've had since writing the book. It also helps with literacy development to "reread" and talk about familiar experiences that are captured in words and pictures.

- Create a lending library for sending Class Conflict Stories home with children so they can share their efforts with parents. Use it as an opportunity to teach parents in a concrete way more about central aspects of your Peaceable Classroom. Send the book home with a letter to parents explaining the idea of conflict stories and why they are valuable. Offer parents suggestions about ways to talk about the stories with their children and ideas about how they might use such stories at home. Talk to children when the books are returned to school about what happened with the books at home.

- Help children also make Class Conflict Stories that tell about conflicts they have successfully resolved. For instance, you might ask each child involved in the conflict and working out the solution to write a page about what they did to solve the problem. You can read and discuss these stories at class meeting and send them home so the children can share their accomplishments with their families.

- When individual children are working on their own books as part of early literacy programs, you can suggest they write about their own personal conflict stories. When doing so, many of the same suggestions for writing class conflict stories will help you. When relevant, use the child's efforts as an opportunity to help extend the child's thinking on conflict resolution issues, for instance, by asking, "I wonder if there is anything else you could have tried to do to solve your problem? Do you want to write or (make a picture) about what you think would happen if you tried using that solution?" As appropriate, you can have children share their completed books with others at a class meeting.

Children's Books: Enriching and Expanding the Content of the Peaceable Classroom Curriculum

The Special Power of Children's Books in Peaceable Classrooms

Children's books can support the curriculum of Peaceable Classrooms in many ways. For instance, they can:

- suggest content for discussions about the Peaceable Classroom issues you and the children are working on;

- bring into the classroom content that expands the children's horizons beyond their immediate experience and exposes them to the wide range of diversity among people beyond the home or school;

- raise a difficult or potentially loaded issue for discussion in a way that distances the children from it and makes it seem less threatening;

- provide salient content for play that substitutes for the content children bring to their play from television;

- offer children specific information and ideas that expand their understanding and behavior around Peaceable Classroom issues—for instance, by suggesting a new way to think about or solve a conflict;

- help you interconnect various curriculum areas and goals—for instance, books foster literacy in children, even as you use them to work on specific Peaceable Classroom content;

- support children's literacy development by engaging them in age appropriate literature that has highly meaningful content and which reinforces the power of the printed word.

Guidelines for Using Children's Books to Promote Peaceable Classroom Goals

There are many ways you can work to enhance the role and impact of children's books in the curriculum:

- **Make children's books a regular and valued part of your school day.** Establish predictable structures and routines with children's books such as having a "reading aloud" time every day, a place for displaying and storing familiar and currently popular books so they are readily available to children, and a safe and comfortable place where children can look at books on their own or in small groups.

- **Try to familiarize yourself with a book before reading it to the children.** This will allow you to identify the meaningful issues in the book and plan informally how you might use the book to raise these issues with the children.

- **When a powerful event occurs in children's lives related to the Peaceable Classroom agenda, try to find books to read that relate in some way to the issues raised by the event.** The books do not necessarily have to deal directly with what happened, but rather, can provide a vehicle for the issue to come up. For instance, after the Columbia Space Shuttle exploded, you might try reading a book about space travel.

- **Have regular give-and-take discussions about books you read aloud to the group.** To the extent possible, plan how you will start the discussion based on the issues you feel the book will raise for the children.

- **Help children bring the content from popular books into other aspects of the curriculum.** For instance, you might put a sheet over a table to help children make a store for pirates like Calvin and Angela did in *Best Day of the Week* by Nancy Carlsson-Paige. Or you might bring a wheelchair to the classroom for the children to use after reading *Arnie and the New Kid* by Nancy Carlson.

- **Read books that seem most meaningful to the children more than once, even many times.** The familiarity that comes from multiple readings can help young children get beyond the more obvious aspects of the book's content and look for deeper and more complex connections and meanings. It can also help the class develop shared meanings and ways of talking about issues together.

- **Read more than one book about the same issue.** This can help children can see the variety of ways that an issue can be presented and handled.

- **Read a book and its sequel or a series of books with the same characters.** This can help children get to know more about a particular character and apply what has been learned about that character through play. For instance, the series of books about "Louie" by Ezra Jack Keats provide a powerful opportunity for children to think about Louie's social and emotional needs, as well as get ideas for creating space trips, puppet shows, and miniature dioramas.

- **Find ways to use familiar or currently popular books in new ways to support the curriculum and goals of your Peaceable Classroom.** Most books can be used in many different ways, so choosing your books from a specific list, like the one below, is often much more work than thoughtfully adapting the quality books you currently use in the service of your Peaceable Classroom goals.

- **Use children's books to build bridges between home and school.** Develop a procedure for children to borrow favorite books overnight and bring in favorite books from home to share with others. Have regular communications with families about special books the class is reading. Place currently popular books in a regular spot near where adults pick-up and drop off children, and encourage children and adults to talk about them.

Selection of Children's Books for the Peaceable Classrooms

Aardema, V. *Bimwili and the Zimwi*. New York: Dial Books for Young Readers, 1992.

___. *Rabbit Makes a Monkey of Lion*. New York: Dial Books for Young Readers, 1993.

___. *Who's in Rabbit's House?* New York: Dial Books for Young Readers, 1999.

Aaron, J. *When I'm Afraid*. New York: Golden Books, 1998.

Aliki. *Feelings*. New York: Greenwillow Books, 1984.

Bach, O. *The Biggest Sneeze*. New York: Caedmon, 1986.

Bang, M. *When Sophie Gets Angry—Really, Really, Angry*. New York: Scholastic, 1999.

Blos, J. and Gammell, S. *Old Henry*. New York: William Morrow, Mulberry Books, 1990.

Bourgeois, P. *Franklin Is Bossy*. New York: Scholastic, 1993.

Burningham, J. *Aldo*. New York: Random House, 2000.

Bynum, J. *Otis*. New York: Harcourt, 2000.

Cannon, J. *Stellaluna*. New York: Harcourt, 1993.

Carle, E. *The Grouchy Ladybug*. New York: Viking, Penguin, 1996.

Carlson, N. *How to Lose All Your Friends*. New York: The Penguin Group, 1997.

Carlson, N. *Arnie and the New Kid*. New York: Puffin Books, 1999.

Carlsson-Paige, N. *Best Day of the Week*. St. Paul, MN: Redleaf, 1998. [See accompanying guide, listed in Chapter 16, *Before Push Comes to Shove* by N. Carlsson-Paige & D. Levin].

DePaola, T. *The Knight and the Dragon*. New York: Putnam, 1990.

___. *Now One Foot, Now the Other*. New York: Trumpet Books, 1991.

Dobrin, A. *Josephine's Imagination*. New York: Scholastic, 1973.

English, K. *Speak English for Us, Marisol!* Morton Grove, IL: Albert Whitman & Co., 2000.

Everitt, Betsy. *Mean Soup*. New York: Harcourt, 1992.

Gauch, P. and Ishikawa, Satani. *Dance, Tanya*. New York: Scholastic, 1996.

Garay, L. *The Long Road*. Plattsburgh, NY: Tundra Books, 1997.

Graham, B. *This Is Our House*. Cambridge, MA: Candlewick Press, 1996.

Havill, J. *Jamaica Tag-along*. Boston: Houghton Mifflin, 1990.

___. *Jamaica and Brianna*. Boston: Houghton Mifflin, 1996.

Heide, F.P., and J.H. Gilliland. *Sami and the Time of the Troubles*. New York: Clarion, 1995.

Heine, H. *Friends*. London: Picture Lions, 1997.

Henkes, K. *Chrysanthemum*. New York: Greenwillow Books, 1996.

___. *Wemberly Worried*. New York: Greenwillow Books, 2000.

Hoban, R. *A Bargain for Frances*. New York: Thomas Y. Crowell, 1993.

Hoberman, M. *And to Think that We Thought that We'd Never Be Friends*. New York: Crown Publishers, 1999.

Hoffman, M. *Amazing Grace*. New York: Dial Books for Young Readers, 1991.

Hutchins, P. *The Doorbell Rang*. New York: William Morrow, 1989.

Isadora, R. *Ben's Trumpet*. New York: William Morrow, Mulberry Books, 1979.

___. *At the Crossroads*. New York: Greenwillow Books, 1999.

Jackson, E. *Sometimes Bad Things Happen*. Brookfield, CT: Millbrook Press, 2002.

Jones, M. *I'm Going on a Dragon Hunt*. New York: Viking, Penguin, 1988.

Jones, R. *Matthew and Tilly*. New York: Dutton, 1995.

Kalmanm M. *Fireboat: The Heroic Adventures of the John J. Harvey*. New York: Putnam, 2002.

Keats, E.J. *Louie*. New York: Scholastic, 1983.

___. *The Trip*. New York: Scholastic, 1987.

___. *Regards to the Man on the Moon*. New York: Four Winds Press, 1987.

Kellogg, S. *The Mysterious Tadpole*. New York: Dial Books for Young Readers, 2002.

Leaf, Munro. *The Story of Ferdinand*. New York: Viking, 1976.

Lionni, L. *Six Crows*. New York: Scholastic, 1988.

___. *Swimmy*. New York: Alfred A. Knopf, 1991.

___. *It's Mine!* New York: Alfred A. Knopf, 1996.

Martin, A. *Rachel Parker, Kindergarten Show-off*. New York: Scholastic, 1992.

MacDonald, M. *Peace Tales: World Folktales to Talk About*. Hamden, CT: Linnet Books, 1992.

McKissack, P. *Flossie and the Fox*. New York: Dial Books for Young Readers, 1986.

___. *Mirandy and Brother Wind*. New York: Alfred A. Knopf, 1997.

McLerran, A. *Roxaboxen*. New York: Puffin Books, 1991.

McPhail, D. *Great Cat*. New York: E.P. Dutton, 1982.

Mendez, P. *The Black Snowman*. New York: Scholastic, 1991.

Naylor, P. *King of the Playground*. New York: Simon & Schuster Children's, 1994.

Piers, H. *Long Neck and Thunder Foot*. New York: Viking, Penguin, 1982.

Popov, N. *Why?* New York: North-South Books, 1996.

Sayre, A. *Noodle Man: The Pasta Superhero*. New York: Scholastic, 2002.

Sieszka, J. *The True Story of the Three Little Pigs*. New York: Scholastic, 1999.

Sendak, M. *Where the Wild Things Are*. New York: Harper and Row, 1988.

Seuss, Dr. [T. Giesel]. *The Sneeches and Other Stories*. New York: Random House, 1961.

___. *The Lorax*. New York: Random House, 1971.

___. *The Butter Battle Book*. New York: Random House, 1985.

Steptoe, J. *Stevie*. New York: Harper Trophy, 1999.

Swope, S. *The Araboolies of Liberty Street*. New York: Clarkson N. Potter, 2001.

Udry, J.M. *Let's be Enemies*. New York: Harper and Row, 1988.

Vulliamy, C. *Small*. Boston: Houghton Mifflin, 2002.

Wildsmith, B. *The Owl and the Woodpecker*. New York: Oxford University Press, 1987.

Wood, A. *Heckedy Peg*. New York: Harcourt, 1992.

Zolotow, C. *The Hating Book*. New York: Harper Collins Children's Books, 1969.

Curriculum Webs: Planning and Keeping Track of Curriculum on a Theme or Topic

Planning and keeping track of curriculum activities that are tailored to all your children's needs and backgrounds, developmental levels, and current experiences poses challenges you would not have to face if you followed a prescribed curriculum. To develop an effective Peaceable Classroom curriculum requires careful organization; keeping track of the overall functioning of the classroom, each activity's progress, and each child's needs, performance, and progress; and making constant decisions about what comes next and how to build upon what came before.

This more open-ended, child-centered, and nonlinear approach can present many pitfalls for a teacher. It is never certain where an activity will go. One topic often flows into the next. Subject areas do not always fit into distinct compartments or activities. Each child contributes and learns ideas and skills unique to him or her, and there are few predetermined sequences or prescribed information to be taught at a given moment. In this era of increasing pressure to formally teach basic skills to young children, an additional burden is often placed on teachers to justify how their Peaceable Classroom curriculum is effectively incorporating basic skills.

Curriculum webs can be a valuable resource in your efforts to build a Peaceable Classroom.[1] They provide a procedure for quickly recording and organizing a great deal of information about a classroom in a visually clear and easy-to-read fashion. They can help you:

- brainstorm ideas for activities around a subject area, topic, or issue that has come up in the classroom;

- see connections between various aspects of your curriculum and classroom;

- achieve a balance between allowing children's input into the curriculum and guiding and directing their learning yourself;

---

[1] For more detailed discussions of curriculum webs in the curriculum development process see "Weaving Curriculum Webs: Planning, Guiding, and Recording Curriculum Activities in the Day Care Classroom" by D.E. Levin in *Day Care and Early Education*, 13(4) (Summer, 1986): 16-19; and "Curriculum Webs: Weaving Connections from Children to Teachers" by S. Workman and M. Anziano in *Young Children*, 48(2) (January, 1993): 4-9.

- develop curriculum in collaboration with other adults such that everyone's ideas can be readily incorporated and discussed;

- keep track of the curriculum you have followed for a specific topic, issue, or skill throughout the year;

- communicate effectively with parents and other school personnel about activities in your classroom.

A Curriculum Web Planning Medical Play

Figure 15.1 is the web the teacher in Chapter 5 used to plan the hospital play in her classroom's dramatic play area. It includes her initial ideas about where to start the curriculum. Once the hospital project began, she circled the items that were covered and modified the web, based on the children's responses and input.

Figure 15.1
MEDICAL PLAY CURRICULUM WEB

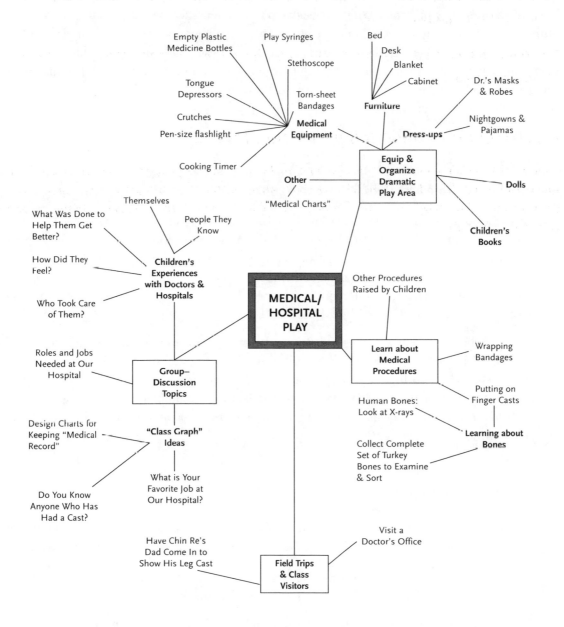

A Curriculum Web Documenting the Use of a Class History Chart

Figure 15.2 is the curriculum web used by the teacher who did the class history chart described in Chapter 10. She developed it several months into the school year to record activities to date and the kinds of learning they promoted. She also used it to record how she was incorporating literacy, numeracy, and social studies into her curriculum. This helped her document for administrators and parents how she was meeting the school's requirements for teaching basic skills within her Peaceable Classroom curriculum. She also used the web to help her explain her curriculum to parents on a special parents' night, and to help other teachers in her school start thinking about using class history charts in their own classrooms.

Examples of Other Ways to Use Curriculum Webs

You can also use curriculum webs to:

- Keep track of and plan for individual children. Include such information as what the child has done, particular needs, and special interests. You can then use another color pen to add on new ideas for what you can try next with that child. Webs like this can also be helpful for planning what to discuss about a child at parent conferences. They can help teaching teams coordinate their efforts with individual children. This is especially true in inclusive classrooms where special needs children are enrolled.

- Brainstorm ways to deal with a problem in the classroom. For instance, the teacher who at a class meeting developed the Helper Chart (described in Chapters 4 and 9) might have first made a quick web, brainstorming possible approaches for dealing with the children's seeming dependence on her. She might then have decided that addressing the problem at a meeting was most likely to accomplish her goals of making the children less dependent on her and more interdependent with each other.

Guidelines for Practice

If you have never used curriculum webs, or have never used them in the open-ended, multi-purpose ways described here, there are a few things to keep in mind that might help you in your efforts:

- **There is no one right set of information for a given web.** The categories you use and information you include should depend on your purposes for making the web.

- **There is not one right place to put each item included in the web.** In fact, most entries could appropriately go in more than one place (and maybe they should).

- **The first web you try is likely to be the hardest.** For many of us it's hard to stop worrying about getting the web right and, instead, focus on using it to brainstorm in a way that helps us quickly collect and organize many useful ideas and information.

Figure 15.2
CLASS HISTORY CHART CURRICULUM WEB

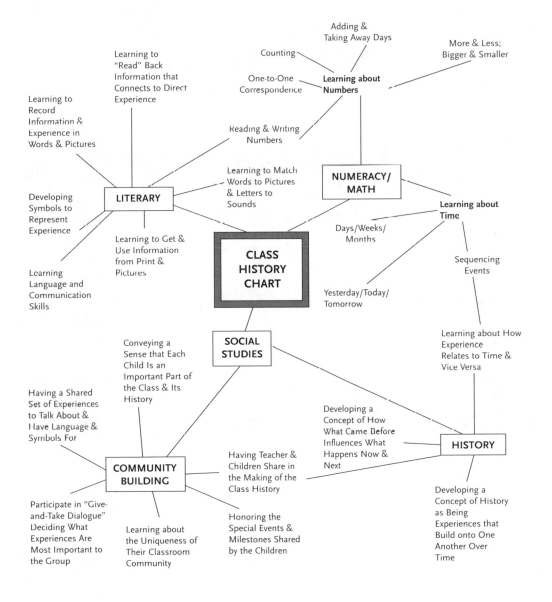

Resources

Books:

American Medical Association. (1996). Physician Guide to Media Violence. Chicago, IL.

American Psychological Association. (1996). *Violence and the Family: Report of the APA Presidential Task Force on Violence and the Family*. Washington, DC.

Apfel, R.J. & Bennett, S. (1996). *Mindfields in Their Hearts: The Mental Health of Children in War and Communal Violence*. New Haven, CT: Yale University Press.

Arnold, J.C. (2000). *Endangered: Your Child in a Hostile World*. Farmington, PA: Plough Publishing.

Arnow, J. (1995). *Teaching Peace: How to Raise Children to Live in Harmony—Without Fear, Without Prejudice, Without Violence*. New York: Berkley Publishing Group.

Ayers, W., Dohrn, B., & Ayers, R. (Eds.). (2001). *Zero Tolerance: Resisting the Drive for Punishment in Our Schools*. New York: The New Press.

Cairns, E. & Dunn, J. (1996). *Children and Political Violence (Understanding Children's Worlds)*. Oxford & New York: Blackwell Publishers.

Canada, G. (1998). *Reaching Up for Manhood: Transforming the Lives of Boys in America*. Boston: Beacon Press.

Canada, G. (1995). *Fist, Stick, Knife, Gun: A Personal History of Violence in America*. Boston: Beacon Press.

Cantor, J. (1998). *'Mommy, I'm Scared!' How TV and Movies Frighten Children and What We Can Do to Protect Them*. New York: Harcourt Brace.

Carlsson, U. & von Feilitzen, C. (Eds.). (1998). *Children and Media Violence. Yearbook from the UNESCO International Clearinghouse on Children and Violence on the Screen*. Gotenborg, Sweden: UNESCO International Clearinghouse on Children and Violence on the Screen.

Carlsson-Paige, N. & Levin, D.E. (1998). *Before Push Comes to Shove: Building Conflict Resolution Skills with Young Children*. St. Paul, MN: Redleaf Press. [See also companion children's book: *Best Day of the Week* by N. Carlsson-Paige in Chapter 14].

Carlsson-Paige, N. & Levin, D.E. (1990). *Who's Calling the Shots? How to Respond Effectively to Children's Fascination with War Play, War Toys*. Gabriola Island, BC, CAN: New Society.

Carlsson-Paige, N. & Levin, D.E. (1987). *The War Play Dilemma: Balancing Needs and Values in the Early Childhood Classroom*. New York: Teachers College Press.

Carter, J. (1994). *Talking Peace: A Vision for the Next Generation*. New York: Dutton Children's Books.

Cecil, N. (1995). *Raising Peaceful Children in a Violent World*. San Diego, CA: LuraMedia.

Charney, R. (2002). *Teaching Children to Care: Management in the Responsive Classroom (Revised Edition)*. Greenfield, MA: Northeast Foundation for Children.

Children's Defense Fund. *The State of America's Children, 2002.* Washington, DC.

Chrisman, K. & Couchenour, D. (2002). *Human Sexuality Development: A Guide for Early Childhood Educators and Families*. Washington, DC: National Association for the Education of Young Children.

Derman-Sparks, L. & the A.B.C. Task Force. (1989). *The Anti-Bias Curriculum: Tools for Empowering Young Children*. Washington, DC: National Association for the Education of Young Children.

Deskin, G. & Steckler, G. (1996). *When Nothing Makes Sense: Disaster, Crisis, & Their Effects on Children*. Minneapolis, MN: Fairview Press.

Developmental Studies Center. (1996). *Ways We Want Our Class to Be: Class Meetings that Build Commitment to Kindness and Learning*. Oakland, CA.

Developmental Studies Center. (1997). *Blueprints for a Collaborative Classroom: Twenty-five Designs for Partner and Group Work*. Oakland, CA.

DeVries, R. & Zan, B. (1994). *Moral Classrooms, Moral Children: Creating a Constructivist Atmosphere in Early Education*. New York: Teachers College Press.

Dyson, A. (1997). *Writing Superheroes: Contemporary Childhood, Popular Culture, and Classroom Literacy*. New York: Teachers College Press.

Eron, L., Gentry, J., & Schlegel, P. (1994). *Reason to Hope: A Psychological Perspective on Violence & Youth*. Washington, DC: American Psychological Association.

Eth, S. & Pynoos, R. (1985). *Post-Traumatic Stress Disorder in Children*. Washington, DC: American Psychiatric Press.

Federman, J. (Ed.). *National Television Violence Study, Vol. 2: Executive Summary*. Santa Barbara, CA: Center for Communication and Social Policy, University of California.

Fox-Keller, S. (1985). *Good Grief: Helping Groups of Children When a Friend Dies*. Boston: New England Association for the Education of Young Children.

Froschl, M., Sprung, B., & Mullin-Rindler, N. (1998). *Quit It! A Teacher's Guide on Teasing and Bullying*. Washington, DC: National Education Association.

Garbarino, J. (1999). *Lost Boys: Why Our Sons Turn Violent & How We Can Save Them*. New York: Free Press.

Garbarino, J. (1996). *Let's Talk about Living in a World with Violence*. Chicago: Erikson Institute.

Garbarino, J. (1995). *Raising Children in a Socially Toxic Environment*. San Franscisco: Jossey-Bass.

Garbarino, J. et al. (1998). *Children in Danger: Coping with the Effects of Community Violence*. San Francisco: Jossey-Bass Publishers.

Garbarino, J. et al. (1991). *No Place to Be a Child: Growing Up in a War Zone*. Lexington, MA: Lexington Books.

Gilligan, J. (1997). *Violence: Reflections on a National Epidemic*. New York: Grosset/Putnam.

Grossman, D. & DeGaetano. G. (1999). *Stop Teaching Our Kids to Kill: A Call to Action against TV Movie and Video Game Violence*. New York: Crown Publishing Group.

Groves, B.M. (2002). *Children Who See Too Much: Lessons from the Child Witness to Violence Project*. Boston: Beacon Press.

Herman, J.L. (1992). *Trauma and Recovery: The Aftermath of Violence from Domestic Abuse to Political Terror*. New York: Basic Books.

Hopkins, S. (Ed.). (1999). *Hearing Everyone's Voice: Educating Young Children for Peace and Democratic Community*. Redmond, WA: Exchange Press.

Hopkins, S. & Winters, J. (1990). *Discover the World: Empowering Children to Value Themselves, Others, and the Earth*. Gabriola Island, BC, CAN: New Society Publishers.

Howes, C. & Ritchie, S. (2002). *A Matter of Trust: Connecting Teachers and Learners in the Early Childhood Classroom*. New York: Teachers College Press.

Kaiser, B. & Rasminsky, J.S. (2002). *Challenging Behavior in Young Children: Understanding, Preventing, and Responding Effectively*. Needham Heights, MA: Allyn & Bacon.

Karr-Morse, R. & Wiley, M. (1997). *Ghosts from the Nursery: Tracing the Roots of Violence*. New York: Atlantic Monthly Books.

Katch, J. (in press). *They Don't Like Me: Lessons on Teaching and Bullying from a Preschool Classroom*. Boston: Beacon Press.

Katch, J. (2001). *Under Deadman's Skin: Discovering the Meaning of Children's Violent Play*. Boston: Beacon Press.

Kohn, A. (1993). *Punished by Rewards: The Trouble with Gold Stars, Incentive Plans, Praise, and Other Bribes*. New York: Houghton Mifflin.

Kohn, A. (1986). *No Contest: The Case Against Competition*. New York: Houghton Mifflin.

Koplow, L. (Ed.). (1996). *Unsmiling Faces: How Preschools Can Heal*. New York: Teachers College Press.

Kozol, J. (1988). *Rachel and Her Children: Homeless Families in America*. New York: Crown.

Kozol, J. (1992). *Savage Inequalities: Children in America's Schools*. New York: Harper.

Kotlowitz, A. (1991). *There Are No Children Here*. New York: Doubleday.

Kreidler, W.J. (1984). *Creative Conflict Resolution: More Than 200 Activities for Keeping Peace in the Classroom*. Glencoe, IL: Scott, Foresman & Co.

Kreidler, W.J. (1991). *Elementary Perspectives #1: Teaching Concepts of Peace and Conflict*. Cambridge, MA: Educators for Social Responsibility.

Kreidler, W.J. & Whitall, S. (1999). *Early Childhood Adventures in Peacemaking: A Conflict Resolution Activity Guide for Early Childhood Educators*. Cambridge, MA: Educators for Social Responsibility.

Lantieri, L. (Ed.). (2001). *Schools with Spirit: Nurturing the Inner Lives of Children and Teachers*. Boston: Beacon Press.

Lantieri, L. & Patti, J. (1996). *Waging Peace in Our Schools*. Boston: Beacon Press.

Leavitt, L.A. & Fox, N.A. (1993). *The Psychological Effects of War and Violence on Children*. Hillsdale, New Jersey: Lawrence Erlbaum.

Levin, D.E. (1998). *Remote Control Childhood: Combating the Hazards of Media Culture.* Washington, DC: National Association for the Education of Young Children.

Levine, M. (1998). *See No Evil: A Guide to Protecting Our Children from Media Violence.* San Francisco: Jossey-Bass.

Macksoud, M. (2000). *Helping Children Cope with the Stresses of War: A Manual for Parents and Teachers.* New York: United Nations Children's Fund.

Mallory, B.L. & New, R.S. (1994). *Diversity and Developmentally Appropriate Practice: Challenges for Early Childhood Education.* New York: Teachers College Press.

Marsh, C. (1999). *Tough Stuff: How to Talk to Kids about Disturbing Contemporary Issues, Including Sex in the White House, Guns at School, Drugs Everywhere, War, and More.* New York: Gallopade International.

Mastellone, F. (1993). *Finding Peace through Conflict: Teaching Skills for Resolving Conflicts and Building Peace.* Amherst, MA: National Association for Mediation in Education.

Miller, G. & Schoenhaus, T. (1998). *Toy Wars: The Epic Struggle between G.I. Joe, Barbie, and the Companies That Make Them.* New York: Random House.

Miller, K. (1996). *The Crisis Manual for Early Childhood Teachers: How to Handle the Really Difficult Problems.* Washington, DC: Gryphon House.

Miller, S., Brodine, J. & Miller, T. (1996). *Safe by Design: Planning for Peaceful School Communities;. Resource and Planning Guide;* and *Resource Supplement.* Seattle, WA: Committee for Children.

Morrow, G. (1991). *The Compassionate School: A Practical Guide to Educating Abused and Traumatized Children.* Englewood Cliffs, NJ: Prentice Hall.

National Association for the Education of Young Children. (Adopted July, 1993). *NAEYC Position Statement on Violence in Children's Lives.* Young Children, 48 (6).

National Association for the Education of Young Children. (Adopted April, 1990). *NAEYC Position Statement on Media Violence in Children's Lives.* Young Children, 45 (5), 18-21.

Obiakor, F., Mehring, T. & Schwenn, J. (1997). *Disruption, Disaster, and Death: Helping Students Deal with Crises.* Reston, VA: Council for Exceptional Children.

Oehlberg, B. (1996). *Making It Better: Activities for Children Living in a Stressful World.* St. Paul, MN: Redleaf Press.

Olweus, D. (1993). *Bullying at School: What We Know and What We Can Do.* Oxford: Blackwell Publishers.

Osofsky, J. (Ed.). (1997). *Children and Youth Violence.* New York: Guilford Press.

Osofsky, J. & Fenishel, E. (Eds.). (1993). *Hurt, Healing and Hope: Caring for Infants and Toddlers in Violent Environments.* Arlington, VA: Zero to Three/National Center for Clinical Infant Programs.

Pelo, A. & Davidson, F. (2002). *That's Not Fair: A Teacher's Guide to Activism with Young Children.* St. Paul, MN: Redleaf Press.

Phillips, C.B. & Derman-Sparks, L. (1997). *Teaching/Learning Anti-Racism: A Developmental Approach.* New York: Teachers College Press.

Pirtle, S. (1998). *Linking Up! Using Music, Movement, and Language Arts to Promote Caring, Cooperation, and Communication—Preschool through Grade 3*. Cambridge, MA: Educators for Social Responsibility.

Polakow, Valerie (Ed.). (2000). *The Public Assault on Children: Poverty, Violence, and Juvenile Injustice*. New York: Teachers College Press.

Pollack, W. (1998). *Real Boys: Rescuing Our Sons from the Myths of Boyhood*. New York: Random House.

Prothrow-Stith, D. & Weissman, M. (1992). *Deadly Consequences*. New York: Harper Collins.

Ramsey, P. G. (1998). *Teaching and Learning in a Diverse World (2nd Edition)*. New York: Teachers College Press.

Ramsey, P. G. (1991). *Making Friends in School: Promoting Peer Relationships in Early Childhood*. New York: Teachers College Press.

Ready by Five Partnership. (1996). *Moving Young Children's Play Away from TV Violence: A How-to Guide for Early Childhood Educators*. Baltimore, MD.

Ready by 5 Partnership. (1998). *Bringing Parents into the Picture*. Baltimore, MD. [To accompany *Moving Young Children's Play Away from TV Violence*.]

Rideout, V., Foehr, U., Roberts, D. & Brodie, M. (1999). *Kids and Media at the New Millennium: A Comprehensive National Analysis of Children's Media Use*. Menlo Park, CA: Kaiser Family Foundation.

Rogovin, P. (1998). *Classroom Interactions: A World of Learning*. Portsmouth, NH: Heinemann.

Scarlett, G. et al. (1998). *Trouble in the Classroom: Managing the Behavior Problems of Young Children*. San Francisco: Jossey-Bass.

Schwarz, T. (1999). *Kids and Guns: The History, the Present, the Dangers, and the Remedies*. New York: Watts Franklin.

Singer, D. (1993). *Playing for Their Lives: Helping Troubled Children Cope through Play Therapy*. New York: The Free Press.

Slaby, R. (et al.). (1995). *Early Violence Prevention: Tools for Teachers of Young Children*. Washington, DC: National Association for the Education of Young Children.

Stamford. B.H. & Yamamoto, K. (Eds.). (2001). *Children & Stress: Understanding & Helping*. Olney, MD: Association for Childhood Education International.

Straus, M. (1994). *Beating the Devil Out of Them: Corporal Punishment in American Families*. Lexington, MA: Free Press.

Terr, L.C. (1990). *Too Scared to Cry: Psychic Trauma in Childhood*. New York: Harper & Row.

Thornton, T. et al. (Eds.). (September, 2000). *Best Practices of Youth Violence Prevention: A Sourcebook for Community Action*. Atlanta: Center for Disease Control and Prevention (Division of Violence Prevention).

Trozzi, M. (1999). *Talking with Children about Loss: Words, Strategies, and Wisdom to Help Children Cope with Death, Divorce, and Other Difficult Times*. New York: Berkley Publishing Group.

Vance, E. & Weaver, P.J. (2002). *Class Meetings: Young Children Solving Problems Together*. Washington, DC: National Association for the Education of Young Children.

Walsh, D. (1994). *Selling Out America's Children: How America Puts Profits Before Values and What Parents Can Do.* Minneapolis, MN: Fairview Press.

Webb, N. (Ed.). (1991). *Play Therapy with Children in Crisis.* New York: Guilford.

Whitney, T. (1999). *Kids Like Us: Using Persona Dolls in the Classroom.* St. Paul, MN: Redleaf Press.

Curriculum and Training Materials:

ACT—Adults and Children Together—Against Violence. An ongoing project providing community-based training for early childhood violence prevention with ongoing materials development. Brochures include: "Understand Child Development as a Violence Prevention Tool" and "Violence Prevention for Families of Young Children." Washington, DC: American Psychological Association & National Association for the Education of Young Children. (www.ActAgainstViolence.org)

Channeling Young Children's Play Away from Media Violence. A five-lesson manual for an adult education course for professionals and parents on counteracting the negative impact of media violence. Companion publications include: *Moving Young Children's Play Away from TV Violence: A How-to Guide for Early Childhood Educators* and *Bringing Parents into the Picture.* Baltimore, MD: Ready At Five Partnership. (www.medialit.org/catalog)

Children and Conflict: An Opportunity for Learning in the Early Childhood Classroom. Videotape and teacher education materials designed for adults working with children 18 months to eight years. Designed by C. French & L. Wirtanen. Boise, ID: Child Care Connections. (www.ccie.com)

Different and the Same: Helping Children Identify and Prevent Prejudice. Series of video-taped scenarios with puppets for working with children on anti-bias issues as well as materials for training teachers to use the program. Pittsburgh, PA: Family Communications, Inc. (www.mrrogers.org)

Early Childhood Adventures in Peacemaking. Educators for Social Responsibility's project designed to connect a child's need for healthy play with conflict resolution education. Successfully implemented in hundreds of centers, AIP combines developmentally appropriate practice with activities that create connections between young children. Cambridge, MA: Educators for Social Responsibility. (www.esrnational.org)

Ready to Learn about Conflict. A video-based training program of the PBS "Ready to Learn" Project designed by Media Education Consultants for training professionals to help parents teach children conflict resolution skills. Washington, DC: Public Broadcasting System. (www.pbs.org)

Re-framing Discipline. A three-part, video-based training program to help teachers of children three to eight transform "discipline problems" into learning opportunities. Beaverton, OR: Educational Productions. (www.edpro.com)

The Safe Havens Training Project: Helping Teachers & Childcare Providers Support Children & Families Who Witness Violence in Their Communities. Video-based training program. Pittsburgh, PA: Family Communications. (www.childcarerockland.org)

Second Step: Violence Prevention Curricula for Preschool through Grade 9. Program with curriculum kits for teaching positive social behavior. Seattle, WA: Committee for Children. (www.cfchildren.org)

Supporting Children in Resolving Conflicts. A videotape on teaching conflict resolution skills to children through helping them work out conflicts when they arise in the classroom. Ypsilanti, MI: High/Scope Press. (www.highscope.org)

What Happened to the World? Helping Children Cope in Turbulent Times. A 65-page booklet prepared by J. Greenman that is packed with information on helping children, from toddlers through elementary school age, cope with the tragedy of September 11th. Also available is the accompanying 75-page Facilitator's Guide for training adults to work with children on these issues. Watertown, MA: R. Russell & J. Greenman. (both can be downloaded from www.brighthorizons.com)

Organizations:

American Academy of Pediatrics. Publishes position statements on various aspects of children and violence. (www.aap.org)

UNESCO International Clearinghouse on Children, Youth, and Media. [Formerly the UNESCO International Clearinghouse on Children and Violence on the Screen.] Publishes extensive free resources on all aspects of media, media violence, and children on a global level and an international directory of activists and researchers. Gotenborg University, Sweden. (www.nordicom.gu.se)

Educators for Social Responsibility. Conducts teacher training workshops and institutes on teaching social responsibility and creating Peaceable Classrooms. Publishes and distributes a comprehensive-range of violence prevention and peace education materials for all school ages. (www.esrnational.org)

Lion & Lamb Project. Parent organization promoting healthy play & nonviolent toys through printed materials, training trainer programs, and advocacy. (www.lionlamb.org)

National Association for the Education of Young Children (NAEYC). Publishes materials on violence and children, including: *Media Violence & Children: A Guide for Parents* (1994, brochure); *Position Statement on Violence in the Lives of Children* (1993, brochure); *Position Statement on Media Violence in Children's Lives* (1990). (www.naeyc.org)

Public Broadcasting System (PBS). Regularly updates materials on its web site to help parents talk with their children about issues of violence. (www.pbs.org/parents)

TRUCE (Teachers Resisting Unhealthy Children's Entertainment). Prepares parent guides on media violence and media-linked toys, which you can download from the web to copy and distribute. (www.truceteachers.org). Teacher booklet, *Help Children See through Violence in the Media* (in English and Spanish), available from the Massachusetts Violence Prevention Task Force. (www.violenceprevention.com)

Acknowledgements

A far-reaching community of colleagues, friends, and family has contributed to the creation of this book. My deep appreciation and thanks go to:

- Karen Economopoulos, whose deep and unfailing respect for children and ground-breaking teaching, contributed immeasurably to my understanding of Peaceable Classrooms and the ideas, conversations, and activities described here.

- Nancy Carlsson-Paige, who in our over twenty-year collaboration during which we wrote four books together, has contributed immeasurably to the ideas and spirit of this book.

- The committed and inspiring educators in elementary and early childhood settings who have contributed many of the best ideas for building Peaceable Classrooms that are presented here, including: Meg Bruton, Lori Churchill, Sydney Gurewitz Clemens, Abby Gedstad, Toni Gross, Judy Kline, Sue Kranz, Kathy Meyer, Sarae Pacetta, Deborah Poklemba, Elizabeth Powers, Ruth Schreier, Lucy Stroock, Megan Thomas, as well as the many other unnamed teachers who have shared examples of their work with children in these difficult times.

- The many parents who so generously shared their amazing stories and experiences of the challenges of raising their children in violent times, including: Randi Beckmann, Bev Bruce, Lori Churchill, Stephanie Cox-Suarez, Lerato Jackson, Pamela Linov, and many more.

- The many, many children who taught me so much about learning to live peacefully in a violent world—as they shared their amazing ability to work out their needs in violent times through play, art, interactions with peers, and conversations with caring adults, including: Chad, Louisa, Addy, Sam, and many, many more. My thanks also goes to the children (and their teachers) at the Daisy Child Development Center, Employees' Center for Young Children, Inc., Fayerweather Street School, Haggarty School, Tobin School, and Shady Hill School. It is these children who helped me believe not only that Peaceable Classrooms are possible, but also that Peaceable Classrooms are what children seek.

- Wheelock College, and my colleagues there, for providing an environment in which this work has been able to grow and flourish for almost too many years to count.

- The many Wheelock College graduate and undergraduate students who were in placements with children on September 11, 2001 and shared with me their stories of what happened at their placements that day. I also want to acknowledge the many other students through the years who have taught me so much from their experiences with children and also the helpful work of Graduate Research Assistants, Liz Kinstlinger and Lisa Thomas, who helped me with many of the classroom examples which were in the first edition of the book.

- The many colleagues who have contributed to my understanding of and ability to respond effectively to issues of violence in children's lives including: the Steering Committee of Teachers Resisting Unhealthy Children's Entertainment (TRUCE) including long-standing members Christine Gerzon, Kathy Roberts, Honey Schnapp, Julie Rivinus, and Janet Schmidt; the Center for Peaceable Schools at Lesley University where I am a research associate; and Early Childhood Education On-line Listserv members who so willingly share their expertise, experiences, and concerns. Also, Diane Trister Dodge, James Garbarino, Betsy McAllister Groves, Susan Linn, Marsha Lovell, and Alvin Poussaint.

- My editor at Educators for Social Responsibility, Jeff Perkins, who has shared in the process of revising this book with every bit as much commitment and care as I brought to the project myself and has provided good advice and unending support. Thank you, Jeff, for making this project such a meaningful and rewarding one for me. And thanks to the others at ESR for the importance they have given to this project, especially Larry Dieringer, whose idea it was to initiate this revised edition and who always based decisions about the book on how to optimize its positive impact on children and schools. Also, Linda Lantieri and Sandy Whittall who bring so much care and expertise, and Sonja Latimore and Laura Parker Roerden, who nurtured and edited the first edition of this book. Thanks also to Toy Reid and Garrett Graddy for their help in the production, as well as Josh Silverman and Ben Spear at schwadesign for their inspired design of the book.

- The National Association for the Education of Young Children, especially my editor there, Carol Copple, for becoming the co-publisher because of her commitment to making the ideas in this book available to its membership and the wider early childhood community. Seeing ESR and NAEYC work together on this project provides a model of the power that can come from a truly collaborative effort.

- William Kreidler, whose understanding of how to help young children learn to work out their conflicts peacefully and generosity in sharing that knowledge, contributed to many of the ideas about conflict resolution in this book. I miss you, Bill, but you have left a unique legacy behind which continues to grow.

- Zell Draz for her friendship and unfailing interest in and very generous support of this work. I miss you, Zell, but your generosity continues to help make my work on projects like this book possible.

- And finally, to my family: my husband Gary, who has always truly valued my passion for doing this work and supported me in my efforts to do it in more ways than I could ever list here; my son, Eli, who kept me grounded in the realities of raising a child in this violent world and who has shown me by his example how the ideas in this book can make a difference in who children become; and my parents, Emma and Arthur, who continue to provide ongoing support and appreciation of my efforts to make the world a better place for children.

Diane E. Levin, Ph.D., is a Professor of Education at Wheelock College in Boston, Massachusetts, where she teaches courses on children's play, media, and violence and runs a summer institute on media education in a violent society. She has also taught in regular and special needs settings. An internationally recognized expert on how violence and media affect young children's development, ideas, and behavior, her work also focuses extensively on what teachers, parents, and the wider society can do to counteract their harmful effects. She is the author or coauthor of six books including *Remote Control Childhood? Combating the Hazards of Media Culture* (NAEYC), *Before Push Comes to Shove: Building Conflict Resolution Skills with Children*, and *Who's Calling the Shots? How to Respond Effectively to Children's Fascination with War Play and War Toys.*

Diane is a co-founder of Teachers Resisting Unhealthy Children's Entertainment (TRUCE), an advocacy group which works to promote nonviolent, creative play and media, and of the coalition to Stop Commercial Exploitation of Children (SCEC). She is a Research Associate at the Center for Peaceable Schools at Lesley University, has served on the NAEYC Panel on Violence in the Lives of Children, and testified at US Senate Commerce Committee Hearings on Marketing Violence to Children. In addition, Diane has consulted with the American Psychological Association's ACT Against Violence Program, Public Broadcasting System children's projects (including as primary advisor on its parents' web site on "talking with kids about war and violence" and for PBS Families Magazine), and the State of Maine, developing statewide training on violence prevention for childcare providers.

Diane can be contacted at: Wheelock College, 200 The Riverway, Boston, MA 02215; dlevin@wheelock.edu.

Index

National Association for the Education of Young Children

Promoting Excellence in Early Childhood Education

naeyc NAEYC is the world's largest early childhood education organization, with a national network of local, state, and regional affiliates. We are more than 100,000 members working together to bring high-quality early learning opportunities to all children from birth through age eight. Membership is open to all who share a commitment to promote excellence in early childhood education and to act on behalf of the needs and rights of all children. For information about membership, publications, or other NAEYC services, visit www.naeyc.org.

If you liked this book, check out these titles from NAEYC!

Remote Control Childhood? Combating the Hazards of Media Culture
Diane Levin

A must-have handbook for reducing media culture's negative impact on children's lives—the heavy doses of violence, stereotyping, commercialism, and the hours spent watching instead of doing. Provides effective guidance and strategies for teachers and parents to minimize harmful media effects and to reshape the media environment that children grow up in. NAEYC order #326.

Class Meetings: Young Children Solving Problems Together
Emily Vance & Patricia J. Weaver.

Have you tried involving children in class meetings for working out the conflicts and problems that arise? It's a great way to build classroom community and promote children's problem-solving skills. The authors' guidance and practical strategies for class meetings are effective with children in preschool through the early grades. Great for bilingual classrooms too! NAEYC order #222.

A World of Difference: Readings on Teaching Young Children in a Diverse Society
Carol Copple, ed.

Antibias, culturally responsive curriculum is not a one-unit lesson or one-time theme, but an approach that pervades curriculum. This collection of thoughtful work addresses a wide range of issues—culture, language, religion, inclusion, socioeconomic status, and more—with emphasis on building respect and understanding. NAEYC order #261.

Educators for Social Responsibility

Creating Schools Where Young People Want to Be and Teachers Want to Teach

esr Educators for Social Responsibility (ESR) is a national leader in educational reform that was founded in 1982. Our mission is to make teaching social responsibility a core practice in education so that young people develop the convictions and skills to shape a safe, sustainable, democratic, and just world. Our work spans the fields of social and emotional learning, character education, conflict resolution, diversity education, civic engagement, prevention programming, youth development, and secondary school improvement. We offer comprehensive programs, staff development, consultation, and resources for adults who teach children and young people preschool through high school, in settings including K-12 schools, early childhood centers, and afterschool programs. For more information visit www.esrnational.org.

If you liked this book, check out these titles from ESR!

Early Childhood Adventures in Peacemaking
William J. Kreidler and Sandy Tsubokawa Whittall

This bestselling guide makes conflict resolution fun! Through games, music, art, drama, and storytelling, young children learn effective nonviolent ways to resolve conflicts. This resource includes sections on developmentally appropriate practice, tips on classroom set-up, instructions for incorporating social and emotional skills into daily routines, and materials to send home to parents to reinforce the concepts of the Peaceable Classroom. (ECHAIP)

Linking Up!
Sarah Pirtle

This teaching guide and accompanying music CD by award winning songwriter and educator, Sarah Pirtle, provides an exciting way to build social and emotional competence in three- to nine-year-olds through music and movement. Featuring hundreds of activities based on 46 easy-to-learn songs that promote caring, cooperation, and communication. Twenty songs are bilingual with lyrics in English and Spanish. (LINKGU)

Changing Channels
William Kreidler, with music by Cathy Fink and Marcy Marxer

This kit will help parents and caregivers counter the possible negative effects of TV and other mass media on young children. Contains music from Grammy-nominated songwriters Cathy Fink and Marcy Marxer; two activity guides by William J. Kreidler; and lists of recommended videos, books, and software. (CHACHA)